Surviving
an Affair

Other books by Willard F. Harley, Jr.

His Needs, Her Needs
Love Busters
Five Steps to Romantic Love
Draw Close
Fall in Love, Stay in Love
Buyers, Renters, and Freeloaders
Effective Marriage Counseling
His Needs, Her Needs for Parents
Defending Traditional Marriage
I Promise You
I Cherish You
Your Love and Marriage
Marriage Insurance
Give and Take

Surviving
an Affair

Dr. Willard F. Harley, Jr.
Dr. Jennifer Harley Chalmers

Revell

a division of Baker Publishing Group
Grand Rapids, Michigan

© 1998, 2013 by Willard F. Harley, Jr., and Jennifer Harley Chalmers

Published by Revell
a division of Baker Publishing Group
P.O. Box 6287, Grand Rapids, MI 49516-6287
www.revellbooks.com

Printed in the United States of America

Library of Congress Cataloging-in-Publication Data
Harley, Willard F.
Surviving an affair / Willard F. Harley, Jr., Jennifer Harley Chalmers.—Revision edition
    pages cm
    ISBN 978-0-8007-1954-8 (cloth)
    1. Adultery. 2. Marriage. 3. Marriage counseling. I. Chalmers, Jennifer Harley.
II. Title.
HQ806.H36 2013
306.73′6—dc23   2013003802

The internet addresses, email addresses, and phone numbers in this book are accurate at the time of publication. They are provided as a resource. Baker Publishing Group does not endorse them or vouch for their content or permanence.

14   15   16   17   18   19   20   8   7   6   5   4   3   2

To Joyce and Phil

Contents

Appendices

1

You Can Survive This Affair

*I*f you are a victim of infidelity, you have been on the emotional roller-coaster ride of your life. Most couples caught up in the tragedy of an affair tell us that they have never felt such intense emotions. They are overwhelmed by anger, depression, fear, guilt, loneliness, and shame.

A betrayed spouse will ask, *How could my spouse do this to me—cheating on me, lying to me over and over again? I can never trust my spouse again. I have so much anger and resentment it scares me. My feelings go way beyond hurt—I can't even put into words the pain I'm feeling.*

A wayward spouse often says, *I used to beg my spouse for more attention but I never beg anymore—my lover gives me all the attention I need. But I don't know if the attention I'm getting is worth the price. One moment I'm sure I've done the right thing. Then I look into the faces of my spouse and children and I'm not sure anymore. I don't want to give up my family, but if I give up my lover I'll be losing the best thing that ever happened to me. What should I do? I'm an emotional wreck!*

When a couple feels such strong emotions, many question if marital reconciliation is possible. *How can we ever recover from such pain? And even if we recover, can we live with the memory of betrayal? Can we ever trust each other again? Can we ever love each other again?*

As marriage counselors we have been asked these questions thousands of times and have been able to respond with a definite *yes*. Let us assure you that if you put into practice what we recommend in this book, the prognosis for the future of your marriage is very good.

In the pages that follow, we use "I" to refer to either of us as we describe our experiences and counsel.

It's Hard to Believe That Marital Recovery Is Possible after an Affair

When I first counseled spouses who were trapped in an affair, I thought I would be preparing them for divorce. But to my surprise, again and again I saw opportunities to save marriages. Infidelity did not necessarily cause either the betrayed spouse or the wayward spouse to want a divorce. Often what they both wanted was to escape the pain of their mistake and create a thriving marriage.

So that became my mission—to help couples recover from the disaster of an affair and create a fulfilling marriage that would prevent any future affairs. Unfortunately, my early attempts to save these marriages failed because I wasn't listening.

In case after case, the unfaithful spouse told me that they had lost their love in marriage and had found it in another relationship. They felt that they had to choose between a passion-filled affair and a loveless marriage. Initially, I ignored the obvious—helping them to create a passion-filled marriage—and instead focused on communication training that did little to create the passion they had experienced in the affair.

The betrayed spouse was equally pessimistic about creating a passion-filled marriage. After going through the worst experience of their life, they certainly were not feeling very passionate. It was all they could do to just hang on for the sake of their children.

Eventually, I came to understand that if I were to save these marriages, I would need to help couples recreate the passion they once had for each other. Once they were in love, the horror of the affair would fade away and the risk of divorce would end.

When spouses are in love with each other, they never divorce. Never! So it certainly makes sense to teach spouses how to fall in love and stay in love with each other. And that's what my program of recovery achieves. If you follow it, I guarantee that you will be in love with each other. And when you are in love, you will not even consider a divorce.

Ever since I began helping these tormented couples fall in love with each other and protect their marriage from any future affair, I've witnessed the recovery of thousands of marriages. But the path that leads to recovery is very narrow, and unless couples follow that path, the tragedy of an affair can permanently cripple a marriage and often leads to the further tragedy of divorce.

If you are a wayward spouse or a betrayed spouse, you may be undecided as to what to do next. One moment you want to divorce your spouse, and the next you want to try to reconcile. That's the way most people in your situation feel because there are advantages and disadvantages to both choices. Divorce carries with it the destruction of a family and the loss of a spouse you may still care for, yet reconciliation means you will be living with the scars of betrayal and the risk of another affair. Your emotional reactions may be so strong that you simply cannot make the choice right now.

> *The path that leads to recovery is very narrow, and unless couples follow that path, the tragedy of an affair can permanently cripple a marriage and often leads to the further tragedy of divorce.*

Even if you have decided that marital reconciliation is impossible, or if it's only you or only your spouse who wants to survive the affair and restore your marriage, I would like you to consider my strategy for recovery. It has proven successful for thousands of couples in hundreds of cultures around the world, and once you understand its objectives, you may be willing to try it. My plan is that narrow path that gets you beyond the affair, helps you make your marriage better than it's ever been, and protects you from future affairs.

You Can Do Better than Survive—Your Marriage Can Thrive

There is hope for the recovery of your marriage, and thousands of couples have proven it. When you complete my program for reconciliation, you will

> *My plan is that narrow path that gets you beyond the affair, helps you make your marriage better than it's ever been, and protects you from future affairs.*

have the marriage you have always wanted—one that is filled with love and compatibility.

But before I tell you about my plan for recovery, you need to know some of the common characteristics of affairs. I want to tell you about Jon and Sue. Their situation may be different from yours, but it illustrates some of the basic elements of most affairs. Like so many couples, Jon and Sue thought it could never happen to them.

2

It Could Never Happen to Me!

Jon and Sue were about to celebrate their eighth anniversary and had good reason to celebrate. They had two healthy daughters and a beautiful home, and Jon had just been promoted to a new position that increased his salary by almost 50 percent. That extra income allowed Sue to cut back on her hours at work so that she could spend more time with their children.

Sue was content with her life. She enjoyed the comfortable home and other luxuries that Jon's income was able to provide. She worked as a part-time special education teacher, allowing her time to do what she loved most—raising her children. But when it came to her relationship with Jon, the romance was gone. Sometimes she daydreamed about the times they had spent talking to each other, showing their affection for each other, and making love with passion and excitement. But with his new job there was no time for that. Besides, Sue's life was enjoyable in so many other ways that she thought she could overlook the loss of Jon's companionship.

Jon was also content. He loved his wife and children and was proud of the quality of life he was able to provide them. His new job was enjoyable and challenging, although it required most of his time. He wanted to spend more time with Sue and his children, but he and Sue had both agreed that their time to be together would come after he was more established in his career.

Jon was an achiever, and Sue loved that trait in a man. In fact, she had married him partly because she knew he was ambitious and would provide well for her and their children. She had encouraged him to accept the responsibilities that led to his advancement. Sue wanted Jon to reach his highest potential but she didn't understand that the time he spent away from her prevented him from reaching his potential as her husband.

On the evening of their anniversary celebration, Sue and Jon exchanged cards and gifts that expressed their love for each other. Then they went to dinner at their favorite restaurant, where Jon had asked Sue to marry him.

But something wasn't right. Sue felt uncomfortable talking to Jon. Their conversation about their children, his work, her work, and even about their plans for the future all seemed contrived and forced. She felt so distant from Jon that it was as if she hardly knew him.

When they returned home, Jon expected to end the evening making love to Sue, but to his astonishment, she was not interested. Jon and Sue had agreed from the beginning of their marriage that sex was never to be a ritual. It was to be an expression of their true feelings, something they did when they both felt a sexual passion for each other. But though Sue and Jon had been out together on their anniversary, Sue still felt lonely and certainly not passionate. When she told Jon she wasn't interested in sex, he went to sleep very disappointed.

The next day Sue felt guilty about the way their anniversary had ended and called her husband three times to tell him how bad she felt. She blamed it all on having been in a bad mood that week and tried to assure Jon that it wasn't anything he had done to upset her. But she was at a loss to know what was causing the problem or what to do about it. The passion was simply gone.

So instead of admitting her lack of feeling for Jon, Sue made love to him the next night, even though she did it because of guilt, not passion. What's worse, she pretended to enjoy the experience as much as she had in the past. She decided that it was unrealistic to have sex with Jon only when she felt passionate.

Sue didn't tell Jon how she now felt about sex. So he assumed that whatever was bothering her on their anniversary had ended and everything was back to normal again. In fact, after their anniversary Sue saw to it that they made love more often than before, which made Jon very happy.

Sue, though, began to feel restless and bored with her life. When a friend suggested that she volunteer for the Lake Restoration Committee, she jumped at the opportunity. Sue and Jon were both concerned about the way development was affecting the quality of the lake that bordered their community. The committee met monthly and Sue enjoyed being part of a group that was doing such important work. She became friends with several of the committee members and developed a particularly good friendship with Greg.

It was so easy for Sue to talk with Greg at the meetings. They usually sat together and he was always very friendly and cheerful. He listened attentively to her ideas, rarely interrupted her, and discussed issues with her in a respectful and supportive way. In fact, he usually came to her defense when others disagreed with her opinions.

Between meetings Greg often called Sue at home to discuss committee business, and once in a while they would meet for lunch. The more she got to know Greg, the more she looked forward to his calls and their lunch dates.

Greg had been divorced for three years and had custody of his two boys, who were five and seven, close to the ages of Sue's children. Sue admired him for the good job he did caring for his children without the help of a wife. But she also felt sorry for him bearing all of the burden himself, so she offered to help him care for his boys if he was ever stuck.

At first, Sue told Jon about her friendship with Greg. When she had lunch with Greg or watched his children in an emergency, Jon knew about it. Jon had lunch with women from work once in a while, so he could not see a problem with Sue having lunch with a man. Besides, he trusted Sue. He believed that she would never be unfaithful to him. And Sue would never have imagined that she could be unfaithful to Jon.

But as Sue's friendship with Greg deepened, she became increasingly secretive about it. She knew that if she were completely honest about how much time she was spending with Greg, Jon would become alarmed and encourage her to put a stop to it. She told herself she had a right to a friendship with a man, and that she could handle it. Besides, Jon didn't usually ask her what she did during the day, so she seldom had to lie. She simply didn't talk about her growing secret life.

Within a few months of Sue and Jon's anniversary dinner, Greg had become more than just a friend to Sue. She had fallen in love with him, and Greg was in love with her. Sue could not remember ever feeling so attracted to a man, not even to Jon. Greg made her feel beautiful, interesting, desirable, and alive.

The secret life, however, could not remain a secret forever. It came crashing into the open when Jon decided to surprise Sue by returning home two days early from one of his many business trips. Sue had arranged to have the children spend the night with her parents so she could be alone. Jon quietly entered the house and went to his bedroom with flowers and candy in his arms. There he found Sue—and Greg! Greg grabbed his clothes and ran out of the house, leaving Sue alone to try to explain what had happened.

The Dangerous Illusion: It Could Never Happen to Me

In their eight years of marriage, neither Jon nor Sue ever thought they would be the victims of infidelity until it actually happened. They had friends who had been unfaithful to a spouse, but Sue and Jon felt they could never betray each other's trust that way and they believed their moral standards set them apart from those who yield to the temptation of an affair.

Spouses who have not experienced an affair firsthand are usually very trusting. They don't believe that infidelity could ever infect their marriage. I often hear, "My spouse could never be unfaithful—she has my utmost trust," and "He has such strong moral convictions that an affair is unthinkable."

Infidelity happens in most marriages.

When a spouse has an affair, it usually comes as a complete surprise even to him or her. That person often reports, "I had always regarded those who had affairs as selfish, misguided fools with no discipline whatsoever. I could not have imagined having an affair myself."

But infidelity is something that doesn't just happen on TV dramas. It happens in most marriages. *Most* marriages, you may ask? Yes, unfortunately, most marriages.

As common as an affair is in marriage, it is always devastating to almost everyone involved. It's one of the most painful experiences that the betrayed spouse will ever be forced to endure, and it is traumatic for the children. Friends and members of the extended family usually suffer as well. But what most people don't realize is that the wayward spouse and the lover are also hurt by the experience. They almost always suffer from acute depression, often with thoughts of suicide. With all of the sadness and suffering, why do so many people have an affair?

The answer is that, for the moment, it seems to be the right thing to do. Men and women are easily carried away by their emotions, making the worst mistakes of their lives.

One would think that at least the people with strong religious convictions and moral commitments would have special protection from extramarital affairs. Yet I have counseled hundreds of people with these convictions who were not able to resist unfaithfulness. Just observing the many religious leaders who have succumbed to the temptation of infidelity proves to me that under certain conditions infidelity is irresistible.

The truth is that infidelity doesn't necessarily develop out of a bankrupt moral values system. Instead, personal values change to accommodate the affair. What had been inconceivable prior to an affair can actually seem reasonable and even morally right during an affair. Many people who have always believed in being faithful in marriage find that their values do not protect them when they are faced with the temptation of an affair.

It became clear to me early in my counseling experience that affairs were much more common than I had ever imagined. Now, after years of marriage counseling, I have come to realize that almost everyone, given the right conditions, would have an affair.

Sue's Side of the Story

I never thought I would be unfaithful to Jon. I had always looked at people who had affairs as moral weaklings. But my view has changed. Now I understand how important it is to be with the one you love, even if your friends and family don't approve. And I have a new appreciation for others who have affairs.

I broke my vow of fidelity and feel very guilty about it. Jon wants to work things out and get our marriage back on track, but I would rather die than leave Greg. I now believe my marriage to Jon was a mistake because I didn't understand what love really is. I never would have married Jon if I had known Greg first. We will be soul mates for the rest of our lives.

I feel guilty and ashamed of what I've done, and even what I'm thinking, but nevertheless my feelings for Greg are powerful and undeniable. I've tried to forget about him but I can't do it. Greg rekindled feelings in me that have been dormant for a long time. I find myself thinking about him often and wish I could always be with him.

Jon is a good man and doesn't deserve what I've done to him. I know he loves me. But I cannot remain married to a man I don't love, even though a divorce would probably be hard on our children. If I were to lose Greg, I would lose my soul and my spirit. He has become a part of me, a part I cannot abandon or ignore. Even if I never see Greg again, he will be in my heart for the rest of my life.

Most unfaithful spouses see an affair as enlightenment. They did not know what they were missing until the affair revealed it to them. In many cases a spouse is feeling depressed and unfulfilled, and the affair changes that. What had been missing in his or her life is found, and it's a wonderful relief. What years of therapy can't achieve is instantly accomplished whenever the lover is present—happiness and fulfillment.

But in some cases a spouse is not depressed prior to an affair. Sue, for example, was content with her life. The only sign of her vulnerability was that she no longer felt like making love to her husband. Her passion was gone, leaving a void that Greg willingly filled.

Sue did not develop a friendship with Greg because she wanted him as her lover. She simply needed a friend. And she never intended for their friendship to develop into an affair. She trusted herself to be faithful to Jon. But Greg did such a good job caring for her that he met her important emotional needs and she fell in love with him.

What made Sue's relationship with Greg seem so right was that it was unplanned. It just "happened." That's why Sue felt that Greg was meant to be her lover, because she had not done anything to encourage it. They simply found each other and when they did, they each thought they had found their soul mate.

Jon's Side of the Story

Jon, of course, was blown away by what he saw when he returned from his trip. He had no idea that Sue was having an affair. It seemed like a very bad dream from which he would eventually wake up. But after a few days passed, he had to face the truth. He had been betrayed by the person he trusted most in life: his wife. She had hurt him more than he could have ever imagined.

When we first married, Sue and I made an agreement with each other that we would always be honest about our feelings. I trusted her and never doubted her word. Now I will never believe a thing she says to me again.

Ever since I've known her, she has cared about the way people feel. She can't even hurt a bug. Yet she has chosen to hurt me, the one she promised to care for the most. I thought I knew her but I guess I never did. How could I have not seen through her deceit? How could I have been so blind?

Sue and I both worked very hard to build a good life for ourselves and our children. I admit that I have not been with her much these past few years. I could have done a better job helping her raise our children, too. But we talked about all of that and she agreed with me that what I was doing was best for all of us. I didn't complain to her about the sacrifices I was making for our future, and she didn't complain to me, either. We just did what we felt needed to be done.

Now I don't know what to think. What gets me is that I had plenty of opportunity to cheat on her, but I resisted the temptation because I would have felt too guilty about it. Apparently she doesn't care enough about me to feel guilty. She can just jump in bed with whoever happens to come along and feel great about it the next day. I just don't know her anymore.

I strongly believe that a husband and wife should have the freedom to have any friend they want, male or female. My wife and I have discussed that in the past and we agree. When she asked me how I'd feel if she had coffee with her friend Greg, I said, "sure." I didn't think anything of it. It was the worst mistake of my life. I can't believe that she fell in love with him. I trusted her. We had an agreement.

As painful as this is, I still love her and I hope we can work this out. At first I wanted a divorce. But now I am willing to fight to win her back, even though I'm not sure she's worth fighting for. She cheated on me! Maybe I should just end all of this now and get a divorce.

Most betrayed spouses are blindsided by the affair. They trusted their spouse and their spouse betrayed that trust. Their feelings swing from wanting a divorce and ending all the misery to wanting to save the marriage at all costs.

The emotional impact of an affair on a betrayed spouse is incredibly powerful. Many cannot sleep for days and experience the worst depression of their lives. At the same time, they are on the verge of angry outbursts, losing their temper whenever they get on the subject of the affair. Their anxiety is also out of control as they panic over where this affair will lead. They see no hope of recovery, their lives totally ruined.

> *The emotional impact of an affair on a betrayed spouse is incredibly powerful.*

The betrayed spouse feels pushed into a pit, crying out for help. The wayward spouse comes to the edge of the pit but instead of tossing a rope, hurls stones. Emotionally torn to pieces, the betrayed spouse can't imagine ever trusting anyone else again, least of all the wayward spouse.

Greg's Side of the Story

There is one other person who is an important part of this drama—the other man. He has a very different perspective on the affair than either Sue or Jon.

My friendship with Sue began very innocently. We worked together on a lake restoration project, and that gave us a chance to get to know each other. I was very attracted to her from the first time I laid eyes on her but I knew she was married and I don't believe in interfering with someone else's marriage. So I was very careful not to make any moves that she would interpret as inappropriate.

But as we talked about our personal lives, I about my ex-wife and she about her marriage to Jon, we found many similarities. My ex-wife had ignored me for years and had pursued a career that may have satisfied her, but it sure didn't take me into account. One day she announced that she was leaving me because she was no longer in love. Now that I look back on my marriage, I'm glad she left because I don't think she ever was in love with me.

Sue's husband had not left her but he may as well have left. He spent very little time with her or the children. All he did was pay the bills. Sue craved attention, and I was willing to give her that attention because I was her friend. I was willing to do the things for her that her husband should have been doing. I helped her with her children, I was there to talk to her whenever she needed to talk, and as our relationship developed, I was able to give her the love and affection that she had been missing in her marriage. I gave her the very things that I had missed in my marriage. And Sue was very grateful.

Our friendship is very real and very right. We are two friends who support each other through good times and bad times. We do for each other what a husband and wife should do—we care for each other.

I don't believe that I am the cause of Sue's marriage breaking up. I think Jon is fully to blame for that. She would be making a big mistake not to leave him because, after the dust settles, he'll go right back to working all the time and leaving her home alone.

Sue and I were meant to be together, and I will wait patiently for Sue's divorce. She is not certain what she wants just yet, but I know she loves me and eventually we will be together.

It would be easy to see Greg as the villain in this tragic story. After all, he was the one who pursued a married woman with children. And yet his motives were not entirely selfish. Greg helped Sue as one friend would help another. In fact he did such a good job helping her that she fell in love with him. As the relationship deepened, he became aware of her loveless marriage. After all, that's how Sue described her marriage to Jon—loveless. So, as a friend, he tried to help her with this problem. Greg's own divorce had led him to believe that people sometimes make bad choices when they marry. He saw his divorce as inevitable. So it made sense to conclude that Sue's marriage was also the result of poor judgment. Sue and Jon were simply wrong for each other, and the sooner Sue left her marriage, the happier she would be.

Jon, Sue, and Greg were surprised by what had happened. But if they had understood how vulnerable people are and how easy it is to fall in love with a good friend of the opposite sex, they all would have predicted Sue and Greg's affair.

The Emotional Attachment Continuum

Sue's love for Greg made their affair particularly threatening to her marriage. But affairs that are sexual do not necessarily lead to the feeling of love. In fact most affairs never do reach the level of emotional attachment that Sue and Greg felt for each other. Why, then, would I select Sue's affair as my main illustration when it is not the most common type?

I have chosen Sue's affair as my primary example because her type of affair makes marital reconciliation seem particularly hopeless. By Sue's own admission, she would have been willing to give up everything in her life for Greg, especially her marriage to Jon. With that attitude, is there anything that can be done to save her marriage? Remarkably, there is still a way to achieve that important objective. And that method for recovery works even better in affairs with less emotional attachment.

Since the affair you are struggling with may not be like Sue's affair, it would be helpful for you to see your type of affair in comparison with others. So I will break away from Sue's affair to introduce a variety of ways that people have affairs. The best way for me to describe them is to show you a continuum that reflects the degree of emotional attachment in each affair. On one end of the continuum are affairs like Sue's with intense emotional attachment—those involved consider themselves to be soul mates. But on the other end of the continuum are affairs with almost no attachment at all. The affair you confront probably falls somewhere between these two extremes.

Emotional Attachment Continuum

One-Night Stand		Soul Mates
Almost no emotional attachment	Moderate emotional attachment	Intense emotional attachment

The One-Night Stand

On one end of the emotional attachment continuum where there is almost no emotional attachment, the "one-night stand" is the most common example. It often takes place when a spouse is away on a trip, or when one has gone out partying without the other spouse. In many cases alcohol is a necessary ingredient for these affairs and it enables people to lose enough of their inhibitions to enjoy sex with a total stranger, or at least someone they don't love. Alcoholics are likely to have many of these loveless affairs during their lifetime. In many cases, they can't even remember who was with them for the night.

"If you're not with the one you love, love the one you're with," is the guiding principle in these affairs. People often begin these short-term relationships in such places as bars and dance clubs. But they can also take place on the job, particularly when a spouse is on a business trip. What begins as a casual working friendship in the morning can end with being in bed together at night.

Many people who engage in short-term relationships become very professional at creating just the right climate for a brief affair. Drinking and dancing usually create the mood, and instinct takes over from there. Both people who participate in a relationship like this usually understand that after the evening is over, there should be no serious effort to build the relationship any further. But a "black book" is usually kept so that a call can be made when it's convenient and the other person might be available for a repeat performance. This happens, not because of an emotional attachment, but because it's easier to get together with someone who already knows you than with a total stranger.

While a one-night stand can be an isolated mistake in an otherwise affair-free marriage, it is more often a habit that is repeated by an unfaithful spouse, sometimes hundreds of times. Once in a while a one-night stand will develop into a deeper relationship, but that's unusual.

Those most likely to engage in one-night stands are people who travel as part of their job—interstate truck drivers, airline pilots, flight attendants, traveling sales representatives, business consultants, actors, musicians, seminar speakers. The advantage to these short-term flings, from the wayward spouse's perspective, is that they meet a momentary need with no further commitment or consequences.

There are other types of emotionless affairs besides one-night stands. A spouse who hires a prostitute is an example, although even relationships with prostitutes can become emotional. Occasionally, people may have a lengthy affair but never form an emotional attachment to the lover. These people usually have difficulty being emotionally attached to anyone.

While a one-night stand can be an isolated mistake in an otherwise affair-free marriage, it is more often a habit that is repeated by an unfaithful spouse, sometimes hundreds of times.

People who derive a great deal of pleasure from flirting may also have emotionless affairs. Their challenge is to attract someone of the opposite sex to boost their self-confidence. They may not intend the flirting to lead to lovemaking; they may just want to see a willingness to make love, proving their ability to attract a lover. If the flirting leads to sex, that often ends the relationship. Then the flirt moves on to someone else.

Soul Mates

At the opposite end of the emotional attachment continuum are relationships in which there is an intense emotional bond. They usually begin as a friendship, with no flirting whatsoever, and certainly not as a one-night stand. Over time the friendship becomes increasingly caring as the partners come to understand each other's emotional needs and learn to meet them. As more and more needs are met with increasing effectiveness, this relationship often becomes so exclusive that it cannot be maintained along with a marriage. Those who separate from their spouse just to "sort things out" are often engaged in this type of affair, unknown to the spouse. The separation allows for the private and exclusive relationship the lovers desire.

Sue and Greg's affair falls into this category of intense emotional bonding. Their friendship began because of their common interests but developed into a mutual ability to meet each other's emotional needs. They did such a good job caring for each other that they had developed an emotional attachment well before they had made love for the first time, so sex was not a primary motivation for their relationship. But once they began making love, it definitely contributed to their feeling that they were soul mates.

Since friendships are the basis of soul mate relationships, it's important to understand how these friendships usually begin. In many cases, a man and woman simply find themselves together because of employment or a special interest. Sometimes they are neighbors or attend the same church.

A friendship develops from a special willingness to care for each other.

Simply being together, however, does not create a friendship. A friendship develops from a special willingness to care for each other. When one needs help, the other is there to provide it. In many cases a friendship develops over time as a mutual willingness to help each other unfolds.

When Greg first joined the Lake Restoration Committee, he needed help understanding some of the issues that were being introduced. Sue met with him after the meetings to answer his questions. They quickly discovered that they held similar views on most issues, and when the committee discussed and then voted on various questions, Greg and Sue could count on each other to support their position.

Greg and Sue's mutual support with committee matters expanded to helping each other with other difficulties they both faced. Their conversations were filled with concern for each other and appreciation for each other's care.

This willingness to help each other created a very deep friendship that existed before either Sue or Greg talked about their feelings for each other. But one night, while they were talking to each other on the telephone, Greg brought up a subject that changed the course of their relationship. He told Sue that he was in love with her. Sue responded that she felt the same way toward him but she didn't want to do anything to threaten her marriage. Unfortunately, it was too late. Their friendship was already threatening her marriage—the affair had begun.

A friendship develops into an affair the moment a man and woman feel love for each other and express that love to each other. It opens Pandora's box, and from that point on, neither person seems to have much control over the future of their relationship. Their growing willingness and ability to care for each other creates a growing emotional dependence. They both come to need each other's care so much that an end to their friendship is unthinkable.

It was several weeks after Greg's expression of love that they actually made love. Sue was very reluctant to have sex with Greg. She had told herself that friendship with him was okay, as long as it was platonic. She believed she should be able to have as many friendships with men as she wanted, as long as they were not sexual. But she became increasingly affectionate with Greg, and soon they openly expressed to each other their sexual feelings. Finally, the temptation became too great. Her first sexual experience with him was the most intense and fulfilling she could have ever imagined. In comparison, she regarded her sexual relationship with Jon as a joke.

But Sue's affair was no joke, and she knew it. She did not want a divorce because Jon and her children didn't deserve it. She appreciated Jon's ambition and success in his career and she knew how much he loved her. She was also afraid that a divorce might tear her children apart emotionally. Most of the time she was able to convince herself that, as long as no one knew about her affair, no one would ever be hurt. But occasionally the fog of her illusion lifted and she saw the tragedy of what she was doing. In those moments of clarity, she often felt so distraught that she considered suicide.

A friendship develops into an affair the moment a man and woman feel love for each other and express that love to each other.

Most affairs like Sue and Greg's begin as friendships. As the friendship grows, out of genuine concern they try to meet each other's needs. When the needs are met, love is created. Then, one tells the other about his or her feelings of love, the other reveals the same feeling of attraction, and the affair is off and running.

Between One-Night Stands and Soul Mates

I have described the opposite ends of the emotional attachment continuum. One-night stands usually involve little or no emotional attachment while those who consider themselves to be soul mates are highly attached to each other. In between these two poles of my continuum lie the majority of affairs, involving various degrees of emotional attachment.

As I will explain later, marital recovery requires a complete separation of the wayward spouse and the lover, and the separation of "soul mates" is quite a challenge. So I have deliberately chosen Sue's affair as my reference example because they are usually the most difficult to separate. I won't ignore one-night stands and affairs with less attachment, but those who engage in them are usually willing to end the relationship without much fuss.

However, whether an affair is a one-night stand, years of intimate friendship with sexual contact, or anything in between, the way to end the affair and restore a marriage is essentially the same. So even though my initial example is the affair of soul mates, the methods I suggest for ending an affair and restoring the marriage should be applied to all affairs.

3

How Do Affairs Usually Begin?

Sue, how could you do this to me? Jon's vision of Sue in bed with Greg was indelibly etched in his mind. He could not stop thinking about it and wanting to talk about it. *What did I do to you that would cause you to hurt me so much?*

At first, Sue tried to shut him up by telling him that her relationship with Greg was over, and that they should stop talking about the past. Jon desperately wanted to believe her. She made love to him almost every night for the first week in an attempt to prove that her affair was over and that she was in love with Jon. In an effort to give a convincing performance, she imagined that it was Greg in her arms.

Jon had asked good questions and he desperately needed good answers. Why did Sue have an affair? How did it ever get started? What are the conditions that set these disastrous events into motion, and once in motion why do they usually spin out of control?

How Could It Happen?

We begin our search for answers to these important questions by looking more closely at the players in this drama: Jon, Sue, and Greg. Each of them helped create the conditions that made the affair possible.

28

Jon's contribution was his failure to meet Sue's emotional needs. He worked long hours away from her and their children because he felt he was building a secure future for them. He didn't realize that his failure made Sue vulnerable to the first caring man to come into her life.

Sue's contribution was her failure to be honest. She did not tell Jon about her loss of passion for him and she was also dishonest about her developing relationship—and passion—for Greg. Her emotions warned her of the disaster that was to come, but she failed to pass that warning on to Jon.

Sue also had inappropriate boundaries around men. She saw nothing wrong with close opposite sex friendships, yet this is how most affairs start. When one emotional need is met in such a friendship, the others are soon to follow.

Greg contributed to the affair by befriending a married woman. At first, he didn't intend for his friendship with Sue to turn into an affair. He simply wanted to help her with her problems. His care for her seemed sensible and completely harmless. But his meeting the emotional needs that Jon had failed to meet caused Sue to fall in love with him.

Affairs meet important emotional needs. That's why, despite the suffering experienced by everyone involved, people become ensnared by them. And emotional needs are so powerful that whoever meets them can become irresistible.

What Are Emotional Needs?

An emotional need is a craving that, when satisfied, leaves you with a feeling of happiness and contentment and when unsatisfied, leaves you with a feeling of unhappiness and frustration. There are probably thousands of emotional needs—a need for parties, chocolate, football on TV, shopping—I could go on and on. Each of us has some of these needs and not others. But there are only a very few emotional needs that, when met by someone of the opposite sex, make us feel so fulfilled and happy that we can fall in love with that person. I call those our *most important emotional needs*. Those are the ones that make us feel the most satisfied whenever they are met and the most frustrated when they are not met.

When a husband and wife come to me for help, I first identify their most important emotional needs—what makes each of them feel the best? Then

I help them learn to meet those emotional needs for each other. If they learn to do it, they create a fulfilling marriage.

By privately discussing emotional needs with hundreds of men and women, I have discovered that there are ten emotional needs that are usually near the top of the list for most people: the need for admiration, affection, intimate conversation, domestic support, family commitment, financial support, honesty and openness, physical attractiveness, recreational companionship, and sexual fulfillment. (See chapter 11 and appendix A for more information about these needs.)

I have also made a revolutionary discovery that has helped me understand why it is so difficult for men and women to meet each other's needs. Whenever I ask couples to list these ten needs according to their priority, men usually list them one way and women the opposite way. The five emotional needs that men tend to place at the top of their list are usually at the bottom of the list for women, and vice versa—the five *most important* emotional needs of women are usually the *least important* of men.

What an insight! No wonder men and women have so much difficulty meeting each other's needs! They are unable to empathize with each other. They feel like doing for each other what *they* would appreciate the most, but it turns out that their efforts are misdirected. What one spouse appreciates the most, the other usually appreciates the least!

Our most important emotional needs are those that make us feel the most satisfied whenever they are met and the most frustrated when they are not met.

Of course, everyone is somewhat unique. While men on average pick a particular five emotional needs and women on average pick the other five, any specific man or woman may pick other combinations. Therefore, I always encourage each spouse to decide what he or she appreciates the most. I never tell people what their emotional needs are. They always tell me. And when those particular needs are met, they will be in love with the one who meets them.

Jon's ambition and his desire to build an attractive lifestyle for his family was not the cause of Sue's affair. The reason Sue was tempted to have an affair was that her most important emotional needs were not considered when Jon made his vocational decisions. He didn't understand how important it was to meet Sue's needs for conversation, affection, and family commitment. By focusing all of his attention on meeting her need for financial support and ignoring her other needs, he left her vulnerable to someone who would meet those other needs. Out of ignorance, he made decisions to achieve their financial objectives at Sue's emotional expense. If he had known how important it was for him to meet Sue's most important emotional needs as he tried to achieve his lifestyle objectives, he would not have made Sue as vulnerable to an affair.

When our most important emotional needs go unmet, we tend to feel somewhat empty and depressed.

When our most important emotional needs go unmet, we tend to feel somewhat empty and depressed. When those needs are met, we feel alive again—fulfilled. While we all may go through life with unmet emotional needs, none of us is very happy with that kind of life. People who feel depressed because of unmet emotional needs may see therapist after therapist in an effort to relieve their feeling of hopelessness, but they find no relief. They take medication to treat their depression, but that only helps relieve the suffering as long as the medication is used. These people often conclude that there's something wrong with them, that their brain is out of whack, that they are psychologically unstable.

But then they meet someone who makes them feel wonderful. It's as if the clouds have lifted and the sun is shining again. This person usually satisfies the unmet emotional needs quite innocently. It may be that the person is genuinely interested in intimate conversation, expresses admiration that is sincere, or provides exciting recreational companionship. When the unmet emotional needs are fulfilled, the results are incredible. The depressed person is instantly cured—as long as he or she continues to have their emotional needs met. If those needs are no longer met, the depression returns.

Some people believe that the lifting of their depression during an affair is a sign from God that they should abandon past relationships and cling to this new relationship. But it's no sign from God. Instead, it's the way our emotions blindly encourage us to spend more time with those who do the best job meeting our emotional needs. If we were to give in to our emotions and chase after anyone who happens to meet our emotional needs at the moment, our lives and the lives of our families would be chaotic in no time. It's very foolish to let our emotions dictate the course of our lives. But unmet needs have a powerful effect—so powerful that people are willing to give up their spouse as well as their children, career, and beliefs to have their emotional needs met.

To show you how unmet emotional needs lead to an affair, I'll let Sue continue to explain her predicament to you.

I'm in a relationship with Greg because I've had serious problems with my marriage, only I didn't fully realize it until now. I have been very unhappy with Jon as a husband, and knowing Greg has made that very clear to me. I used to think I had a good marriage, but that was because I never knew what a romantic relationship could be.

> The power of unmet emotional needs explains why people are willing to give up their spouse as well as their children, career, and moral values to have their emotional needs met.

Greg and I became good friends very innocently. I was not looking for a replacement for Jon, but my friendship with Greg has shown me what I've been missing all these years. I feel I have turned a critical corner. Greg doesn't earn as much money as Jon but he is very smart and creative and organized, and a fun person to hang out with. He's not as good looking as Jon, but I find him more attractive anyway.

Greg and I had worked together on our committee for months without any thoughts of a romantic relationship. When we first met, I never would have guessed in a million years that I would someday be in love with him. But one day we both realized that we felt something for each other.

Greg makes me weak with desire, something I haven't felt in years. We actually talk and look at each other. It seems so natural, like the right thing to do. When we make love it's like heaven. We see each other several times a week but we must be very careful now that Jon knows about us. We joke and laugh and even have very deep conversations about my marriage problems.

Feeling such pleasure and enjoyment from just his company, let alone the intense passion I feel kissing him, makes me realize just how little I was getting from my marriage. I don't want to ruin my kids' lives. They would resent me forever. But I can't lose Greg either. How would I ever be able to find someone else like him?

There are many things about Jon that I admire. In many ways, he's a great guy. I just don't love him. There's no way that he will ever be what I need in a man.

Affairs Satisfy Emotional Needs

Regardless of where an affair falls on the emotional attachment continuum, it exists because it meets important emotional needs. While it's true that in some cases the emotional needs met in an affair are also met in marriage, in most cases they are unmet in marriage, which makes the affair particularly tempting.

When spouses are temporarily separated from each other, either overnight or on extended assignments, their emotional needs are temporarily unmet and they will often be tempted to find someone else to meet them. So it should be no surprise that careers requiring a couple to be separated are highly associated with infidelity.

The same temptation faced by spouses who are separated also exist for spouses who are together in the evening yet fail to meet each other's emotional needs. Such failure can be due to a high-stress life where both spouses are trying to juggle work with childcare and other responsibilities. They find no time or energy to meet each other's emotional needs. But someone they know on the job, who gives them their time and attention, fills the void. For them, an affair is almost irresistible.

But I have also witnessed some spouses who have not been separated by their careers and whose emotional needs have been met in marriage, yet they have an affair anyway. While meeting each other's important emotional needs greatly reduces the chance of an affair, sadly, it does not completely eliminate it. This type of affair is a testament to the incredible, and often irrational, power of emotional needs.

There Are Reasons for an Affair, but No Excuses

Time and time again, a betrayed spouse will tell me that their unfaithful spouse's affair was the worst experience of their life. In one case a wife told me that it was worse than the loss of her child; in another case, worse than a rape she had endured. A loss of a house by fire, an amputated limb, and many other tragic experiences don't usually compare with the pain suffered by infidelity. On a scale of all other sources of suffering in life, infidelity usually tops the list. And yet, I've found that affairs are very common. I estimate that at least 60 percent of all marriages experience infidelity.

While it's true that unmet emotional needs make an affair more tempting, the suffering that it causes puts the responsibility for avoiding it squarely on the shoulders of each spouse. At the time of their marriage they promise to be faithful, to avoid the worst threat to each other. So if either spouse violates that promise, that person is solely responsible for the offense. A betrayed spouse is never to blame for an affair.

In my explanation of how affairs happen, I'm simply acknowledging the fact that unmet emotional needs make a spouse more vulnerable to the temptation of an affair. And some of us are vulnerable even if our emotional needs are being met. Yet temptation and vulnerability are not excuses for the worst offense a spouse can make. It's the one who commits the harmful act itself who bears all of the responsibility.

Later in this book, I will describe ways to protect each other from your predispositions to have affairs, even when your emotional needs are not being met. But for now I want to make it completely clear that no one deserves to experience the suffering that an affair creates. The only person responsible for an affair and its painful consequences is the unfaithful spouse.

Jon failed to meet Sue's emotional needs because he did not understand how important they were to her. He was putting all of his energy into a career that he thought would make their whole family happy. He was usually too exhausted when he got home from work to meet Sue's emotional needs for conversation and affection. Because these were important needs that were left unmet, Sue was vulnerable to Greg, who was able to meet needs that Jon did not.

But Jon didn't deserve the suffering that Sue's affair inflicted on him. Whatever Sue gained by her affair was inconsequential compared to the pain she caused her husband. Her affair was the most selfish act she could have ever committed against him.

The Feeling of Love, a Powerful Emotion That Should Not Be Ignored

Unmet emotional needs usually provide the temptation to set an affair into motion. But what really complicates the situation is the way we can be affected by those who meet our most important emotional needs—we fall in love. And it's the feeling of love that usually causes affairs to spin out of control.

Initially, when Jon discovered Sue's affair, she was willing to end her relationship with Greg and she tried to avoid seeing or talking to him. She even gave up her position on the Lake Restoration Committee to get him completely out of her life. But her emotional attachment to him was very strong. All she could think about was being with Greg. She missed the way he met her important emotional needs, but there was more to it than that. She was in love with him.

Love is a very powerful emotional reaction. It's love that usually motivates us to marry someone. And it's love that keeps us happily married. But it's also love that makes ending an affair extremely difficult.

Love certainly determined Sue's conduct, especially after her affair was discovered by Jon. When asked why she couldn't leave Greg, she answered, *I love him.* Was that it? Was Sue willing to risk her husband's happiness and her children's future simply because she was in love? I'm afraid so. Her love for Greg was all it took to throw her life and the life of her family into chaos.

How did Sue come to love Greg? And why didn't she love Jon anymore? My concept of the Love Bank helps explain what creates and destroys the feeling of love.

The Love Bank

You and I have within us a Love Bank, and each person we know has an account in it. The Love Bank helps us keep track of the way people treat us. When people do things that make us feel good, "love units" are deposited, and when they do things that make us feel bad, love units are withdrawn.

Suppose someone makes you feel comfortable when you are together. *Ka-chink*, a love unit is deposited into their account. If you feel good with that person, two love units might be deposited. Feeling *very good* might warrant a three-unit deposit. Or if the person does something that makes you feel so good you are likely to remember it for several weeks, four love units might be deposited. You can see how someone who is consistent in making you happy could eventually accumulate quite a large account in your Love Bank. And the higher a person's account is, the more emotionally attracted you are to that person.

But just as people can deposit love units, they can also withdraw them. Someone who makes you feel uncomfortable will withdraw one love unit from their account. If that person makes you feel bad, two love units are withdrawn. Feeling *very bad* results in the loss of three love units. And if you feel so bad you will remember the experience for a while, four love units will disappear from the account. If someone withdraws all the love units he or she ever deposited and then goes on to drive the account deeply into the red, you find you are repulsed by that person.

The feeling of attraction to someone is the way our emotions encourage us to spend time with people who treat us well. When someone makes us happy, our emotions associate that person with happiness, and we want to be with him or her. Similarly, when someone makes us consistently unhappy, our emotions usually tell us to avoid that person.

> *The feeling of attraction to someone is the way our emotions encourage us to spend time with people who treat us well.*

When a certain threshold in the Love Bank is reached with someone of the opposite sex—say a thousand love units—the emotional reaction we call romantic love is triggered. It's not just *attraction* that we feel, it's *incredible attraction*. We don't simply *like* the person, we are *captivated by* the person. We feel wonderful when we are together and often feel terrible when apart. The feeling of love is unmistakable and overwhelming.

As long as your account in someone's Love Bank stays above the romantic love threshold, he or she will be in love with you. So how can a couple keep their Love Bank balances high enough to experience romantic love? By making large deposits regularly. And the best way to do that is to meet each other's most important emotional needs. Unless couples meet those needs, their love for each other cannot be sustained throughout life.

Unfortunately, when a Love Bank balance drops below the romantic love threshold, a siren does not go off, warning us of the danger. Instead, we simply lose the feeling of love we had for our spouse. This loss of love is usually regarded as the normal settling in of marriage partners to a more mature relationship. But actually it is the beginning of serious trouble.

Jon let his account in Sue's Love Bank fall well below her romantic love threshold. He stopped meeting her emotional needs, and over time, all of the love units he had deposited during their courtship and early marriage drained out. On the other hand, Greg's account in her Love Bank soared well over her romantic love threshold. He met the needs that Jon failed to meet and deposited love units every time he was with Sue. The result was that she loved Greg and didn't love her husband, Jon.

The feeling of love that Sue had for Greg, and her loss of love for Jon, made marital recovery very difficult. Greg had a huge emotional advantage over Jon. Whenever Sue was with Jon, his low Love Bank balance made her feel uncomfortable, so she really didn't care to be with him that much. On the other hand, Greg's Love Bank balance made her feel terrific. So she looked forward to every moment they could be together.

As long as Greg kept his Love Bank balance high by continuing to meet Sue's emotional needs, Jon's efforts to make Sue happy would pale in comparison. It's very difficult for a person with a depleted Love Bank account to compete with someone with an overflowing account. Jon came to understand his disadvantage all too well in the months ahead.

4

How Do Affairs Usually End?

Sue's attitude toward Jon would not have given him much hope for their marital reconciliation. But Sue had not told Jon how she felt about him—and how much she loved Greg. Instead, after Jon discovered her in bed with Greg, she told Jon that the affair was over and that she wanted to be reconciled to him.

But Jon was devastated.

I found my wife having sex with another man, in our house, in our bed. After all the crying and all the whys, we had a long talk. She told me how sorry she was for hurting me and how she wanted to be with me for the rest of her life. Some of the reasons she gave me I understood and I was at fault. I can admit my mistakes. These mistakes or errors that I have committed will be addressed and fixed. I do love her with all my heart. In fact sometimes I feel I love her too much.

This hurt, though, is hard to handle. I can forgive her and I think I do forgive her, but my problem is not the forgiving; it's the forgetting. I keep seeing her in bed with the other man. It just pops into my head all the time—there are so many things that make me think about it.

Sue wanted to go away for the weekend, just the two of us. At first I was so excited by the thought of spending the weekend with her. And then I

remembered what she looked like in bed with another man. I made up an
excuse why we couldn't go.

Last night she wanted to have a dinner at a very romantic restaurant.
There was soft music and candlelight. I was enjoying myself for most of
the evening; then the vision of her in bed with the other man popped into
my head again. I told her I wasn't feeling well and we left. In the car she
asked me what was wrong. I couldn't talk about it because I was ready
to cry again. I know that I will eventually get through this but I've never
been so sad in all my life.

For the betrayed spouse an affair is, without a doubt, one of life's most
painful experiences. Jon reacted the way most people react when they
discover that their husband or wife has had an affair. The pain seems
unbearable. The person you trusted the most hurts you in the worst way
possible.

Jon was devastated by what Sue had done. But if he had known Sue's
true feelings, he would have been even more upset. Sue was lying to him,
trying to convince him that things would soon be back to normal again.
But in reality, the worst was yet to come.

In the week following the discovery of her affair, Sue did everything she
could to convince Jon that their marriage was on track again. In a way, she
did want her marriage to work. But his lukewarm response to her efforts,
combined with her love for Greg, gave her little hope for recovery, and she
became very depressed. To make matters worse, Jon announced that he
would be gone for two days on an emergency business trip. He apologized
for the timing but claimed he had no control over the decision. Sue felt that
she was back to square one, married to a man whose career came first and
who would never be able to meet her emotional needs.

The first night that Sue was left alone, she was filled with an overwhelming sense of emptiness, fearing that she was destined to live her life without
her soul mate. The more she thought about her hopeless future, the more
desperate she became. Finally, she could no longer take it. So she did what
she had promised Jon she wouldn't do—she called Greg.

As soon as Greg answered the telephone and she heard his voice, Sue's
depression was completely lifted. She felt energized and alive again and

knew at once that she could not live without him. Greg had missed her, too, but told her he didn't want to interfere with her marriage and that their future was up to her. Before the conversation ended, they made plans to see each other again, but this time they had to be more careful.

A Secret Second Life Enables an Affair to Grow

For an affair to grow, it usually needs to be kept secret from the unsuspecting spouse. So a secret second life is created to nurture an affair. When married couples tend to lead independent lives and do not pay much attention to each other, that secret second life is easy to create. But when a husband and wife live a more integrated life, it requires much more deception.

Jon and Sue had quite innocently developed independent lives. Since Jon worked so many hours, Sue had interests, activities, and friends that Jon knew nothing about. She hadn't tried to keep them from him—she often tried to tell him about her day, but he didn't show much interest in her activities. She eventually stopped trying to tell him about them. Then, when her relationship with Greg started to develop, she deliberately left information about him out of her conversations with Jon. She even started to lie about where she was and what she was doing so that Jon would not get suspicious.

Sue actually began lying to Jon about the time she spent with Greg long before the relationship had turned into an affair. Deep down she knew that their friendship was getting out of control but she did not want it to end. When Jon asked about what she had done on a given day, she lied occasionally to avoid telling him that she had been with Greg.

After Jon knew about their affair, Sue and Greg conspired together to deceive him. Sue would park her car at a shopping mall, and Greg would pick her up so that if Jon went looking for her, he wouldn't find her car near Greg's house. Sue made telephone calls to Greg from pay phones, just in case Jon was tapping her home phone or getting her cell phone records. She called Jon at work just before getting together with Greg to give Jon the impression that she was home alone. Whenever she was with Greg, she created a believable story for Jon.

40

Often unfaithful spouses, like Sue, do not have a history of lying, but their affair turns them into masters of deception. Once in a while the fog will lift, and they see how dishonest they have become. When that happens, they usually panic and recognize the affair for the mistake it is. But eventually the fog comes back, clouding their judgment, and they go back to their lifestyle of cheating and lying.

> *Unfaithful spouses do not necessarily have a history of lying, but their affair turns them into masters of deception.*

Throughout their marriage, Sue and Jon had allowed free access to each other's personal information, and that understanding made Sue's effort to deceive Jon very stressful for her. She felt obligated to answer his questions about her whereabouts whenever he asked, and that meant she always had to prepare a lie to explain each time she was with Greg.

Since Jon and Sue had a history of being honest and open with each other, it was not easy for Sue to maintain her secret second life. So she tried to change the way she and Jon related to each other. She no longer wanted to be open with Jon and asked him to respect her privacy.

How Spouses Keep a Second Life Secret

"Stay Out of My Private Life!"

One of the most common clues that an affair is going on is an unfaithful spouse's unwillingness to let the other spouse know about all aspects of his or her life. If a spouse refuses to talk about the events of the day, it may be a sign that a secret second life exists. When an unfaithful spouse makes his or her life a private matter, off-limits to the betrayed spouse's inquiries, the secret second life is difficult to discover.

In an effort to improve honesty and openness, I asked one couple to share with each other their email passwords and access to their voicemail. The husband refused, claiming that everyone should have some privacy in life. My request was so threatening to him that he stopped meeting with me. I warned his wife that his secrecy could be due to an affair and that she should investigate that possibility. Weeks later she discovered that her husband was indeed having an affair.

When you stop to think about it, privacy doesn't improve marriages. It's honesty and openness that improve marriages. The more information you have about each other's thoughts and activities, the easier it is to meet each other's needs and resolve conflicts. Privacy actually blocks access to that important information, and that ultimately leads to marital failure.

As long as Jon was free to ask Sue about every aspect of her life, deception was a full-time job. She had to concoct a story every time she saw Greg, which was very often. As time went on, she realized that it would be much easier to carry on her secret second life if she didn't have to always account for her whereabouts.

Privacy doesn't improve marriages. It's honesty and openness that improve marriages.

She told Jon that one of the reasons she didn't love him as much as she should was because he violated her right to privacy. He overstepped his boundaries and didn't give her a chance to breathe. She said she would love him much more if he would back off and let her have some privacy, not having to always account for her whereabouts.

Jon didn't buy Sue's argument for privacy. He had already seen evidence of lies, and when she asked for privacy, he suspected that she might be back with Greg.

"I'm Disappointed That You Don't Trust Me"

Another way Sue tried to defend her secret second life was to appeal to trust. When Jon raised questions about her suspicious activities, Sue often expressed shock that he could be so distrusting as to even ask these questions. She tried to make it seem as if such questions were incredibly disrespectful. Sue believed that the best defense was a good offense, and so she tried to make Jon feel guilty whenever he asked questions regarding her activities.

One day Jon came right out and asked Sue the obvious question, *Are you still seeing Greg?*

Sue fired back, with shock, anger, sarcasm, and sadness: *How can you think that of me after how hard I've worked to get our marriage back together? For all my effort, this is all I get. Unless you can put what I did behind you, I'm afraid we don't have much of a future together!*

Then with righteous indignation, Sue stomped out of the room. She followed it up by not speaking to Jon the rest of the day and she didn't make love to him for a week. Her strategy worked because it meant she didn't have to pretend that everything was okay between them, and it kept Jon from asking her any more questions about Greg.

The I'm-disappointed-you-don't-trust-me tactic throws the betrayed spouse off balance, making him or her feel guilty and hesitant to pursue the issue. But it kept Jon from asking questions for only about a week. Eventually he saw the strategy for what it was: an effort to protect Sue's secret second life. So he went back to asking questions again.

"I Can't Remember"

Most of us can remember what we did last night. Even if we have to take some time to think of it, we can generally give pretty specific information. And a week later, if we are asked, we are able to provide essentially the same report. But if we were to lie about what we did last night, we would find it surprisingly difficult a week later to remember exactly how the lie went.

If I suspect that a client is lying to me, I ask for specific information, and record it carefully. Then I ask again and again, each time recording what the client says. If the person is telling me the truth, each description of the event is essentially the same. But with a lie, the description changes each time it is repeated.

Jon used the same tactic to uncover lies, and eventually Sue knew what he was doing. So she used another common defense: "I can't remember."

When a person is having an affair, he or she often prefers to provide no information about the secret life, lest someone ask for the story to be repeated, or even worse, check it out. I have encouraged many spouses to ask their husband or wife where he or she has been and what he or she was doing. If the response is, "I really can't remember," it sends up a red flag. Of course the person can remember. They're simply not willing to reveal the truth.

As soon as Sue began using her poor memory as a defense, Jon tried to confront her, saying that her memory for events had been very good in the past. But she insisted that her marital problems had been so upsetting to her that her memory was affected.

"We're Just Friends"

It was an innocent discovery on Jon's part. A business associate happened to mention that he had seen Sue that day. With a few questions Jon learned that she was having lunch with a man that fit Greg's description.

Since many affairs are with friends, it's often difficult to distinguish between an affair and an innocent friendship. Friends and lovers often do the same things—have lunch together, talk on the telephone, send notes, and give each other gifts. A neighbor, a married friend, a coworker, a personal trainer, a professor, a student, a pastor, anyone with whom there is repeated contact and needs are being met, can be a friend—or a lover.

Friends usually meet emotional needs, and love units are deposited when needs are met. So it's easy to understand why friends of the opposite sex would fall in love. Once the friends are in love, the friendship can then be used as an excuse for being together, particularly when there is no hard evidence of an affair.

But in Sue's case, even though Jon had that hard evidence when he found Sue and Greg in bed together, she tried to use the defense that they were now just friends.

Jon didn't believe her, of course, and Sue instinctively reverted back to her shock, anger, sarcasm, and sadness. *My affair with Greg is over, but that doesn't mean we can't be friends. Do you expect me to live in a cave all my life?*

Again, with righteous indignation, Sue stomped out of the room, did not speak to Jon the rest of the day, and wouldn't make love to him. But this time her strategy did not work. Jon knew that her affair was on again and he was very angry. After he regained his composure the next day, he demanded, again, that she stop seeing Greg. Sue told him that he was being controlling and paranoid.

"I Just Need Some Time Away to Think Things Through"

When a spouse asks for a separation to "think things through" or to "decide how I feel," it's often his or her way of getting together with a lover more conveniently.

Sue had grown tired of trying to live a life of deception. She knew that Jon was now on to her, and it would be almost impossible to continue seeing Greg without Jon knowing about it. So she began making plans for a separation.

Moving in with Greg was out of the question. It was one thing for Jon to think she was having an affair, but quite another for him to know about it with certainty.

Asking Jon to leave his home and children was also a problem for Sue. How could she hurt him that much, when he had done nothing to deserve it? Having an affair was bad enough, but Sue didn't think she could live with herself if she took Jon away from his children.

So she decided to look for an apartment where she would live by herself for a while. From there she could visit her children at home as much as she wanted and she would be free to be with Greg without being under Jon's watchful eye. It seemed like the perfect solution.

Since many affairs are with friends, it's often difficult to distinguish between an affair and an innocent friendship.

After she found a place to live near her home, she waited for Jon's next interrogation, and she didn't have to wait very long. As they were eating dinner as a family, he innocently asked Sue what she had done that day. Sue looked him in the eye and said, *It's none of your business.*

It certainly is my business, Jon responded, and that's all Sue needed.

Sue got up from the table. *I've had just about enough of your jealousy and control. I can't take it anymore.*

Then she announced that she would be moving out the next morning.

Her children were heartbroken. They could not understand why she would leave them, but she promised to come back as soon as she was "feeling better." She told Jon the same thing.

Sue had done what she had been dreaming about doing for months—leaving Jon so she could be with Greg. She was free.

As soon as Sue moved into her apartment, she called Greg, inviting him over. This was the day she had planned—moving to her own place and having a private evening with Greg. It was wonderful being with him, but she missed her children terribly. She hadn't expected that, and after Greg left, she cried herself to sleep.

An Affair Is an Illusion

Until her separation, whenever Sue was with Greg, she was almost always happy because he met some of her most important emotional needs. Her conversation with him was enjoyable and interesting, and he always gave her his undivided attention when they talked to each other. He showered her with affection, continually giving her assurance that he loved her and would always be there for her if she needed him. He also had a great sense of humor, another thing missing in her life with Jon.

Sue's relationship with Greg had been essentially free of conflict. They deliberately avoided any unpleasant subjects when they were together. It was as if they were living in a kind of bubble, protected from the cares of normal living. So they rarely argued about anything.

The special world that Sue and Greg had created maximized their Love Bank deposits. They spent their time together meeting each other's emotional needs and avoiding anything that would upset the other. So many love units were deposited that they had left the romantic-love threshold far behind. Their balances were so high that they believed their love for each other would last forever.

But the conditions that had made Sue's affair so enjoyable for her were created at Jon's expense. Sue and Greg had very few conflicts because Jon was shouldering many of the mundane responsibilities of Sue's life. It was his work and his income that gave Sue the quality of life she enjoyed and the freedom to create the conditions that made her affair work. She had her part-time job, childcare available to her when she needed it, and the ability to come and go as she pleased.

Separation was about to change all of that.

With Separation Comes a Glimpse into Reality

When Sue was with Greg after she left her family, all was not a bed of roses anymore. She began to doubt whether she had done the right thing. All she could think about was how her children looked at her when she left them. Even Greg could not cheer her up, and that was the beginning of trouble for their relationship. Until then, they always had fun together, but after the separation, it wasn't fun anymore. Sue began to experience Love Bank withdrawals.

During the first week of separation from Jon, Sue spent as much time with Greg as she could. But she discovered almost immediately that having Greg as a lover was very different than it would be having him as a husband. Of course, he wasn't her husband yet, but she began thinking of him in those terms. Being away from Jon helped her realize how much she had depended on him for things she took for granted, and how Greg simply wasn't able to fill his shoes entirely. He would never be able to earn the income that Sue had come to expect and he would never be the real father of her children. Jon and Sue had created a very comfortable lifestyle together, and as she sat in her apartment, she began to miss it terribly.

Before the separation, whenever Sue and Greg talked about their future together, they would imagine how wonderful it would be. But they had never actually worked out the details. Now they were faced with the reality of it all. When they tried to plan Sue's divorce, all she could talk about was her guilt and depression. Greg grew impatient with her and they began to argue with each other. Lovemaking just wasn't the same after such conversations. Withdrawals were made from both of their Love Banks.

Sue believed that the way she felt about Greg was a sign that they were meant to be together. She didn't understand that it was Greg's balance in her Love Bank that made her feel the way she did. And the only reason he was able to deposit so many love units was that they had created a lifestyle insulated from the problems of everyday life. But as soon as she left Jon, the bubble was broken.

It wasn't long before Sue's intense feelings of love for Greg began to change. And without her passion for him, she was able to begin to see the reality of her world—a husband who loved her, children who needed her, and a lifestyle that was the envy of everyone she knew. What could she have been thinking?

The fog had lifted, and Sue called Jon. He was so glad to hear from her that he could hardly talk. When she asked him how he'd feel if she returned home, he was ecstatic. By the end of the day, she was with her family again.

But within a week, Sue was back in her apartment again. She had missed Greg terribly and couldn't stop thinking about him. She had talked to him several times by phone, and that was all it took to redeposit many of the love units that had been lost. Once again she was crazy about him, and the illusion of the affair completely possessed her. She couldn't remember the guilt and depression she felt when separated. All she could think about was living the rest of her life with Greg.

Sue wasn't back in her apartment a day before the fog lifted again and she saw the mess she was making of her life. The depression she felt was so severe that she started to think about suicide as the only way out of the terrible trap she had created. But instead of killing herself, she made an appointment with a counselor to help her think things through.

Sue's new counselor suggested that her depression was caused by separation from her children. To help her overcome the depression, the counselor encouraged her to ask Jon to leave their home so she could return. She had been resisting that plan because she didn't want to hurt Jon any more than he had already been hurt. But she had become so depressed that in desperation, she took the counselor's advice and asked Jon to leave his home, which he reluctantly agreed to do.

Living at home with her children, however, did not alleviate Sue's depression. In fact her feeling of hopelessness seemed to intensify, so antidepressant medication was prescribed to help her cope with the pain.

Sue saw Greg regularly, but the good feelings she previously had when they were together became increasingly difficult to create. She felt a great deal of guilt and depression in spite of the therapy and the medication she was taking. Greg wanted her to file for divorce and marry him, but Sue resisted the idea. Deep down she knew that he was not what she wanted as a husband. He was great in the insulated bubble they had created during their affair, but in the real world, she saw huge problems on the horizon. Her children were very unhappy about the prospect of her divorce, and she knew that Greg would never be able to provide the standard of living she had come to enjoy. Already, when she had asked Greg for financial help, she found that he was not the generous man she had known when she didn't need much. As their conflicts multiplied, their fights escalated.

There were many issues that seemed to pop out of nowhere. For example, the care of her children became a point of contention. During their affair, they tended to ignore her children when they were together so that they could give each other undivided attention. But now she ignored Greg when she was with her children. Their time together was no longer insulated and carefree. Instead, they spent their time trying to address the real problems that Sue's separation had created.

Greg really didn't have what it took to make a good husband for Sue because he lacked the ability to meet some of the needs that Jon had been meeting. On the other hand, Jon could learn to meet the needs that Greg had met, if Sue would give him a chance. It was only Sue's feeling of love for Greg that maintained her illusion that they would be great together. But they were really not that compatible, and by living in the real world together, that truth would be revealed to her.

Sue's behavior took a great toll on her account in Jon's Love Bank. All of the deposits she had made over the years of their marriage together were cascading out of his Love Bank. Eventually, he lost his love for her.

But before the year had ended, Sue and Jon's relationship got the break it needed. Sue discovered that Greg had developed a friendship with another woman. Up to that moment, Sue was very confused. She loved Greg, but couldn't imagine marrying him. That perpetual state of stress left her in constant emotional turmoil, but she couldn't let go.

When she found out that Greg was cheating on *her*, however, the light dawned. It made a lot of sense to her that a man who was willing to be part of her affair would also be willing to cheat on her. Greg was no longer the knight in shining armor that she had loved and respected. After a fight to end all fights, where she called him every name in the book, and he responded by telling her that he had never thought much of her either, their relationship finally came to an end. Greg told Sue that he was in love with the other woman, someone without a husband or children, and he encouraged Sue to return to her husband.

Even after all that, Greg's decision to leave her was devastating to Sue. She cried, begged him to reconsider, and threatened suicide. But too many love units had been withdrawn already, and he had lost his love for her. Her desperation withdrew even more, and it became hard for him to remember what he had ever seen in her.

Immediately after her fight with Greg, Sue, in desperation, called Jon and invited him to return home to her. He graciously accepted.

As soon as Jon moved back to their home, he found Sue to be as depressed as he had ever seen her. She slept all day and could hardly eat anything. The entire experience had just about destroyed her.

Affairs Usually Die a Natural Death

At some point, almost all affairs that are exposed to the light of day die a natural death. In fact, I've found that over 95 percent of affairs end within two years of having to face reality. If they remain in secret, however, they can go on for decades.

In some cases, it's the lover who ends the relationship, finding that the wayward spouse isn't living up to expectations. And in other cases, it's the wayward spouse who ends it, when the disadvantages of the affair begin to outweigh the advantages. Regardless of who ends the affair, it usually happens when the affair becomes more trouble than it's worth.

Affairs rarely survive because they are usually based almost entirely on emotion. There is rarely a logical reason for having the affair. In fact, they rarely make any sense at all. Careers are often in ruin, finances are set in disarray, and moral values are abandoned. The children's future is thrown to the wind, as is everyone else who has come to trust the unfaithful spouse. An affair is one of life's most bizarre and destructive human temptations.

But there's yet another reason that affairs rarely survive: they are based on dishonesty and thoughtlessness. The same self-centeredness that creates an affair is also responsible for its destruction, because no relationship can survive long without honesty and thoughtfulness. When a couple having an affair start to treat each other the way they've been treating their spouses, the emotional forces keeping it together break apart. And without emotional glue, there's no reason to stay together.

5

How *Should* Affairs End?

Sue's affair with Greg ended the way most affairs end—it died a natural death. Once an affair is exposed to the realities of life, the protective bubble usually breaks and the passion fades away. Without passion, the stupidity of an affair becomes painfully apparent to everyone involved, and the only emotion left is depression of the worst kind.

The affair was bad enough for Jon, but the way it ended seemed even worse. Greg left Sue. Only then was she willing to have Jon come back home. Jon had won her back only because Greg was no longer interested in her.

However, there are couples who follow a different path when an affair is discovered. They are spared much of the pain and suffering that Sue and Jon endured in the months following the exposure of her affair. And their marital recovery is much easier because they ended their affair the right way.

How *should* an affair end? Lee and Kevin's experience is a good example of how it should be done.

Kevin and Lee's Story

Hey, Kevin, what's up? As Kevin's friend and coworker, Amy knew something was wrong.

Oh, it's nothing, probably just the forty thing, Kevin responded, referring to the fact that he had just turned forty. He had a great job as manager of an auto dealership, and had four beautiful children. But he was unhappy with the way his life was turning out.

His discontent was with his wife, Lee. She had changed, and Kevin wasn't sure why. She had always been there for him, with encouraging conversation and affection that seemed to have no limits. Lee had also looked sensational, and they used to have a wonderful sex life together. Unfortunately these were all just memories.

Kevin noticed a change in Lee when their first child was born. He knew that children would require adjustments in their lifestyle, but he never thought that a child would create such a transformation in Lee's attitude toward him. Before their child arrived, Kevin seemed to be her highest priority in life, but after the child, he seemed to be her lowest priority.

Their second child made matters even worse. All the love and affection that Lee had given to Kevin during the first years of their marriage were now refocused on their two children. As two more children arrived, Kevin and Lee's relationship continued to deteriorate.

Lee was a good mother and gave her children excellent care. She kept them clean and well fed, helped them with homework, and was their chauffeur to music lessons, sports practice, and church events. But her self-sacrificing care for the children kept her in a constant state of exhaustion. She knew something was lacking in her relationship with Kevin but she was simply too busy and too tired to give it much thought, let alone do something about it.

Amy knew that Kevin hadn't been his happy-go-lucky self for some time and she was concerned about him. *You seem to be really down about something, Kevin. I'm a good listener*, Amy said, encouraging him to confide in her.

In the next two hours, Kevin poured his heart out. Nearly in tears, he explained how depressed he had been lately. He just didn't feel like doing much of anything anymore, and had little enthusiasm for life. He also mentioned how his relationship with Lee had suffered over the years—how low he was on her list of priorities.

Amy listened attentively. Trying to help, she suggested that he might start an exercise program with Lee as a way of rebuilding their relationship and his health, all at the same time.

I started working out at the health club last month. It sure has made me feel better. I could get you two free passes if you'd like, she offered.

Wow! Kevin thought. *That does sound like a good idea. Maybe that's all Lee and I need—a little time together.*

That night Kevin told Lee about the passes and suggested they plan to go out together at least twice a week. But Lee did not share his enthusiasm. *I really wouldn't want to leave the children alone at night. But it might not be a bad idea for you to go. It might make you feel a little better if you got some exercise.*

So Kevin decided to work out twice a week—with Amy. The exercise made him feel much better, and it wasn't long before he increased it to three times a week, then four, and finally he met Amy almost every day. He lost fifteen pounds, built endurance and muscle tone, and had not felt so good in years. Each morning he could hardly wait to meet Amy for their morning workout.

Lee encouraged Kevin to go to the health club every morning because she could see how much healthier and happier he had become. But she didn't realize that Amy was exercising with Kevin. It wasn't that Kevin had lied about it—the topic of his exercise partner simply never came up.

It wasn't long before Kevin and Amy had fallen in love with each other. It was predictable, because they spent the most enjoyable moments of each day together. They were both able to conceal their emotions fairly well at first. But it was only a matter of time before the truth was revealed.

One day when Kevin and Amy were together, he brought up the subject of her husband, Al. It was quite an innocent question: *How is Al doing these days?*

Amy became very quiet. Suddenly tears streamed down her face. When she regained her composure, she told Kevin for the first time what a bitter disappointment Al had been to her. She had always hoped to have children and raise a family, but from the time they were married, he had been unable to keep a job and was unemployed most of the time. It was up to Amy to pay most of the bills. If that wasn't bad enough, to entertain himself he spent most of his time with friends who had as little ambition as he had. When Amy came home from work, he was usually nowhere to be found. She had lost her love for him and had already seen an attorney to file for divorce.

Kevin gave her a hug as she cried. Amy hugged him back and then gave him a kiss. Their kiss expressed what they had been secretly feeling for each other for weeks. Neither of them wanted it to stop.

When Kevin came home that evening, Lee could see that something was wrong. He seemed very aloof. That was unusual. He was almost always cheerful and talkative, playing with the kids and chatting with her. Tonight he had nothing to say.

Lee was alarmed by the sudden change in Kevin's mood, and wanted to know what it was all about. At first, Kevin tried to lie to her, saying that it had been a disappointing day at work. But Lee knew that disappointing days didn't affect Kevin that way. He was able to leave his work behind him. So she pressed on and kept asking him questions about what had happened that day to upset him so much. Finally, he admitted to her that he was in love with another woman.

Lee was stunned and then became angry. But she was able to compose herself and, as calmly as possible, she asked Kevin to tell her all about it. Reluctantly, he did. He explained how unhappy he had been in their marriage and how Amy had become someone who really seemed to care about him. She had become his best friend, and now he was in love with her.

I was able to talk to both Kevin and Lee the next day. During our session together, they explained the circumstances that led them to my office, and then I pointed out what had not yet happened to them—Kevin had not yet made love to Amy. He had not yet created a secret second life to give himself greater opportunity to be with her. He had not yet decided to separate from Lee and his children. He had not yet found that Amy wasn't really the woman he wanted after all. And he had not yet begged an extremely resentful Lee to give him another chance after almost destroying her life. Kevin knew that if he stopped his relationship with Amy now, he could avoid all the tragic events that would accompany the continuation of their affair.

The feeling of love is one of the most powerful emotions we ever experience, and it's very difficult to leave someone you love. Yet that's exactly what Kevin had to do—and he had to do it immediately.

Ending All Contact—The Right Way to End an Affair

Although Kevin was in no position to bargain, he tried anyway. Like others in his position, he tried to keep Amy in the loop somehow. You'd think that an unfaithful spouse would be so aware of his or her weakness and so aware of the pain inflicted that he or she would be thoughtful enough to make every effort to avoid further contact with the lover. Instead, the wayward spouse often argues that the relationship was "only sexual" or was "only emotional, but not sexual" or some other peculiar description to prove that continued contact with the lover would be okay. In Kevin's case, he argued that it was "only emotional."

Most betrayed spouses intuitively understand the danger and demand that all contact with a lover end for life. Permanent separation not only helps prevent a renewal of the affair, but it is also a crucial gesture of consideration to the betrayed spouse. After an affair has been exposed, each contact made with a lover feels like a knife in the back to the betrayed spouse. With that reality in mind, and the real danger of an affair rekindling with even casual contact, there is no good reason for the unfaithful spouse to ever see or talk to the former lover. There should be absolutely no contact.

> *Permanent separation not only helps prevent a renewal of the affair, but it is also a crucial gesture of consideration to the betrayed spouse.*

In spite of career sacrifices, friendships, and issues relating to children's schooling, I recommend with all seriousness that there be a sudden and complete end to an affair. And I recommend extreme measures to ensure total separation for life from a former lover.

The Addictive Power of an Affair

Several years ago, I owned and operated ten chemical dependency treatment clinics. At first, we used several different treatment strategies. For some, we tried to encourage moderation, and for others, we tried to achieve total abstinence. It wasn't long before all the counselors agreed that total abstinence was the only way to save drug or alcohol addicts from their self-destructive behavior. Unless they completely abandoned the object of their addiction, the addiction usually returned. For these people, moderation was impossible. The conviction that their drug of choice was off-limits to them for life helped end their cycle of addiction-treatment-addiction.

My strategy for ending an affair with total separation from the lover developed after my experience treating alcoholics and drug addicts. And, over the years, I've found my total-separation strategy to be very effective in ending affairs in a way that makes marital recovery possible. Without total separation, marital recovery is almost impossible.

An affair is a very powerful addiction. The craving to be with the lover can be so intense that objective reality doesn't have much of a chance. The fact that a spouse and children may be permanently injured by this cruel indulgence doesn't seem to matter. All that matters is spending more time with the lover. That makes it an addiction.

> *Without total separation, marital recovery is almost impossible.*

Even the one-night stand may be an addiction. It may not be an addiction to a particular lover, but it may still be an addiction—to one-night stands. In affairs that have low emotional attachment, the addiction is often to the act of having a romantic relationship rather than to a particular lover.

The addiction to one-night stands can also grow from a need to be continually assured of one's attractiveness. People who indulge in such practices want to feel that they can have anyone they want, even that person over there sitting at the bar.

The analogy between a chemical addiction and an affair is striking. In both cases, the first step toward recovery is admitting that the addiction is self-destructive and harmful to those whom the addict cares for the most— his or her family. After recognizing the need to overcome the addiction, the next step is to suffer through the symptoms of withdrawal. Addicts are often admitted to a hospital or treatment program during the first few weeks of withdrawal to ensure total separation from the addicting substance. The longer the separation, the less craving addicts feel. Eventually they regain control of their lives.

The best way to overcome an addiction is tried and proven—abstain from the object of addiction. Alcoholics, for example, must completely avoid contact with any alcoholic beverage to gain control over their addictive behavior. They must avoid places where alcohol is likely to be found, such as bars and parties. They must even avoid friends who drink occasionally in their presence. They must surround themselves with an alcohol-free environment. In the same way, when an unfaithful spouse separates from the lover, extraordinary precautions must be taken to avoid all contact with the lover—for life.

Of course, my advice is not easy to implement. Many people who have had an affair try but fail to make a drastic and decisive break with their lover. In the case of Sue and Jon, Sue managed to be separated from Greg for about a week but couldn't resist talking to him. So her affair continued until it finally died a natural death, leaving pain and suffering in its wake.

But while total separation is not easy to implement, there are ways to make it work. I helped Kevin and Lee create such a plan.

How to Tell a Lover That the Relationship Is Over

How can I explain to Amy that I will never see her again? Kevin asked. The answer to that question is an extremely important part of the plan to separate. Kevin needed to end the relationship in a way that would make their separation complete. And he also needed to do it in a way that would be least offensive to Lee.

But Kevin's instincts would not have led him to the correct procedure. If left to his own devices, he would have taken Amy on a Caribbean cruise to say their final good-byes. At the very least, he would have wanted to take her to a secluded spot and discuss the pros and cons of their future together. From Kevin's perspective, he would want to let her down gently, and end the relationship with care and concern for her future. After all, he had encouraged her to love him, and now he felt he had no right to abandon her with no warning. Besides, he wasn't just in love with her, he cared about her, too. She was his best friend.

The approach Kevin would have used to end the relationship not only would have been very offensive to Lee, but it probably would have failed. I've witnessed many of these "final" good-byes and there's nothing final about them. All they do is leave the unfaithful spouse and the lover even more convinced that they belong with each other.

From Lee's perspective (and mine), Amy was the worst enemy of Kevin and Lee's marriage. She stood in the way of their happiness and the happiness of their children. Lee did not want Kevin to "let Amy down gently."

I recommended to Kevin that he write Amy the final good-bye in a letter. I did not want him to see or talk to her ever again if at all possible.

The letter had to be written in a way that was acceptable to Lee. It was to be short and to the point. It was to begin with a statement of how selfish it was to cause those he loved so much pain, and while marital reconciliation cannot completely repay the offense, it would be the right thing to do. Then Kevin would explain how he cared about Lee and his children, and for the sake of their protection had decided to completely end his relationship with Amy. Kevin would promise never to see or communicate with Amy again in life and would ask Amy to respect that promise. Nothing would be said about how he would miss her.

At first Kevin felt that such a letter would be a cruel way to end his affair. But he eventually understood how important it was to completely close the door on any hope of a future relationship. It was over, and Amy needed to know that. If Kevin had given Amy any false hope, preventing her from moving on in her life, it would have been incredibly cruel.

Kevin wrote this letter to Amy and let Lee read it:

Amy, I want you to know that out of respect and love for my wife and children, I have come to realize that I must never see or talk with you again. My relationship with you was a cruel indulgence that Lee did not deserve. While I cannot completely repay Lee for the pain I have caused her, I will do my best to become the husband she has been missing. I care a great deal for my family and I would not want to do anything to risk their happiness. I will not make any further contact with you and I do not want you to make any contact with me. Please respect my decision to end our relationship.

Sincerely, Kevin

A mutual friend was asked to deliver the letter to Amy so that there would be no opportunity for Kevin to add anything to its content. I told Kevin that he should not call Amy. It's very tempting for an unfaithful spouse to tell the lover that the letter is not entirely his or hers, but rather one that the spouse and counselor wrote.

Extraordinary Precautions Must Be Taken to Guarantee No Contact

An affair is not only extremely destructive to a marriage, but it is also extremely difficult to end. So Kevin's willingness to end his relationship with Amy had to be reinforced with extraordinary precautions that would make it difficult for them to contact each other again.

The extraordinary precautions that I recommend focus special attention on conditions that made the affair possible. Many of the couples I've counseled have added precautions to this list because, for them, those conditions were instrumental in making the affair possible. But in general, these precautions help make a rekindling of the affair, and the possibility of future affairs, much less likely.

1. Block Communication with a Lover

Even when a family has moved from one coast to the other, email, texting, and internet social networks are readily available to make contact with a former lover. After the sacrifice of a job change or physical relocation, unfaithful spouses have been known to keep an affair alive.

One man I counseled had ended his affair and was two months into marital recovery when his ex-lover sent him an email. That was all it took to reignite the flame of their relationship, making it more intense and discreet than ever.

Since these forms of communication are a tempting way to make contact with an ex-lover, measures should be taken to make them difficult to use for that purpose. I suggest that a couple use an unlisted home number, change their email address and cell phone number, close their internet social network accounts, and have the betrayed spouse monitor all voice messages, mail, and email. Most important, I suggest that the betrayed spouse have free access to records of all communication including telephone calls and email. These precautions may make an unfaithful spouse feel like a convict on probation, but they are often essential conditions to breaking the addiction that keeps an affair alive.

At first Kevin didn't think such extraordinary precautions were needed. He felt strongly that Amy would not try to contact him once he broke it off with her. But he had his phone number changed anyway. Lee listened to all recorded telephone messages and opened his email to make sure he did not receive any messages from Amy.

It didn't take long before these precautions were proven to be justified. Within two weeks Lee discovered a letter from Amy. In it she told Kevin how much she missed him. Lee told Kevin about Amy's letter but did not describe the contents. They both agreed that Lee should destroy the letter, which is what she did. That experience helped Kevin see how important it was for him to follow my extraordinary precautions.

2. Account for Time

In order to maintain a secret second life, which is an essential ingredient for most affairs, an unfaithful spouse must be able to spend at least some of his or her time away from the watchful eye of the betrayed spouse. So to end a secret second life, it's important to do whatever it takes to assure that time is accounted for throughout the day and night. That's especially true when an affair is first discovered and the unfaithful spouse is willing to end it.

I suggested to Kevin and Lee that they give each other a twenty-four-hour schedule of their daily activities. With the schedule, there would be a telephone number where they could be reached. I explained that it was something they should have been doing throughout their marriage out of consideration for each other. Knowing where Kevin was twenty-four hours a day and being able to contact him also helped Lee restore her trust in Kevin.

I also suggested that they call each other several times during the day, just to talk, but also for Lee to be assured that Kevin was where he said he would be.

Kevin and Lee began giving each other daily schedules. Kevin actually looked forward to Lee's calls. He was also pleasantly surprised when she stopped by his office. He enjoyed getting the attention he had missed during most of their marriage.

When Kevin left the office each day, he called Lee so she would know when he would be home. It was something he should have done throughout his marriage, but he just never got into the habit. What started as a way for Lee to check up on Kevin soon became a way for them to show their care and concern for each other.

3. Account for Money

A secret second life depends not only on hidden time but also on hidden money. Lee usually didn't know how Kevin spent their money, and so it would have been easy for him to divert some of his income to a secret second life.

A secret second life depends not only on hidden time but also on hidden money.

As Kevin and Amy were developing their relationship, he took her to lunch and bought her token gifts. He wasn't spending a lot of money, but he wouldn't have been able to hide the expense from Lee if she were involved on a daily basis in managing their finances.

Kevin had given Lee very little financial information. He earned the money and paid the bills. He gave her an allowance for groceries and incidental expenses, and the rest was his to do with as he pleased. So my suggestion that he make all financial decisions jointly with Lee seemed at first like punishment.

Granted, accounting for how he spent his money was partially intended to be a precaution to help Kevin avoid contact with Amy, but even more important, accounting for money was essential in helping Kevin and Lee build a strong and caring marriage. It wasn't punishment at all—it was the foundation of a thoughtful relationship, in which the money they spent would be mutually beneficial. Eventually Kevin also saw it that way.

4. Spend Leisure Time Together

Kevin and Amy had become each other's best friends partly because they spent much of their leisure time with each other. They not only exercised together every morning, but they also had lunch with each other and often spent time together after work.

We have already discussed the importance of accounting for time, especially leisure time. But another extraordinary precaution that an unfaithful spouse and betrayed spouse should take is to spend their leisure time together.

So I encouraged Lee and Kevin to be together whenever he was not at work. Lee now realized that it was vital to their relationship that she spend more time with Kevin. By using day care and a friend with whom she exchanged babysitting duties, Lee was often able to join Kevin for lunch. They also joined a new health club and exercised together three mornings a week.

Once in a while Kevin was required to take a business trip. Since I encouraged them to spend all their leisure time together, Lee went along with him. They were curious to know how long this extraordinary precaution would be necessary, since it was expensive and inconvenient for Lee to travel with Kevin every time he was gone overnight. My response was that the risk of an affair was too great to ever take any chances. Besides, after they had traveled together for a while, they would probably want to do it the rest of their lives.

5. Change Jobs and Relocate, if Necessary

As long as Amy and Kevin would have worked together, the goal of no contact would have been impossible to achieve. So Kevin had to take the extraordinary precaution of trying to find another job where he would not be working with Amy. Kevin's management job would be difficult to give up, especially since Lee was a stay-at-home mom. She had been out of the workplace for quite a few years and would not be able to earn much even if she were to get a job right away.

I suggested to Kevin that he speak with his boss at work and explain his situation. As it turns out, the auto dealership was one of several owned by the same man, so Kevin was able to move laterally to a similar position at another dealership. But many of the people I counsel do not have such an easy time making a job change. They must take vacation time to look for other work and sometimes remain unemployed for months before a suitable new job becomes available.

Most unfaithful spouses don't think they need to quit a job or move to a new location. They feel they have themselves under control and this extraordinary precaution is unnecessary. Sometimes they insist on a trial period where their commitment can be tested. But a trial period is just an opportunity for the affair to reignite.

> *Easy access to a former lover must be avoided at all costs.*

Changing jobs or moving to a new location is usually a difficult and costly choice. Yet it can be done, and without this extraordinary measure, the risk of an affair spinning out of control is very great. Easy access to a former lover must be avoided at all costs.

Of course, if Amy had decided to quit her job voluntarily, then Kevin would not have had to change jobs. I've seen many cases in which, after an affair is exposed, the lover is the one who moves away, and then it is not necessary for the spouse to change jobs or relocate.

Sometimes a couple will decide to relocate even if the lover has left the area. After the agony of an affair, it's often very helpful to move to new surroundings and start over. Otherwise, everything they see and do keeps reminding them of the affair.

6. Avoid Overnight Separation

Since infidelity is highly associated with careers that separate a husband and wife overnight, I advise couples to choose careers that keep them together. In Kevin and Lee's case, there were instances when Kevin was asked by his employer to attend a conference or auto show that was out of town. Kevin and Lee agreed to attend these events together.

But what if he had been an interstate truck driver, away from home a week at a time? Would Lee have had to travel with him cross-country?

It's been done! Some betrayed spouses I've counseled have made the decision to ride with their spouse to avoid affairs as an extraordinary precaution. In fact one enjoyed the experience so much that when her husband died unexpectedly, she tried to marry another trucker so that she could continue the lifestyle she had come to enjoy. But in cases where a betrayed spouse is not willing or able to travel, I recommend that the unfaithful spouse change careers so that they can be together every night.

Being together at night is not only an important way to hold an unfaithful spouse accountable, but it also eliminates one of the reasons that affairs are tempting. When spouses are not together physically, they are unable to meet some of each other's most important emotional needs. Even one night away from each other can be enough to create a tempting situation.

7. *Allow Technical Accountability*

While it may sound paranoid to those who have never experienced an affair, I'm an advocate of using modern technology to help account for a spouse's whereabouts and what they do on their computer. Global Positioning Systems (GPS) have been used to help discover an affair (which I strongly encourage), and it can be used after an affair is over to help spouses keep track of each other. In addition, key logger programs allow a spouse to see every keystroke and every internet site that has been visited.

These forms of technology help both the betrayed and the unfaithful spouse. They help a betrayed spouse regain trust by being able to test the truthfulness of the unfaithful spouse's reports. The unfaithful spouse is helped by being given additional motivation to resist a relapse, knowing that his or her activities are being recorded.

It took awhile for Kevin to get used to having his life read like an open book. And Lee was not accustomed to checking up on him. But over time, as they learned how to become transparent to each other, they came to regard this extraordinary precaution as valuable. Instead of viewing it as an invasion of privacy, they saw it as a natural way to learn more about each other.

8. *Expose the Affair*

As with addictions, an important part of relapse prevention is to let others know about your weaknesses and gain support for the intended life path. I recommend including family members, clergy, and/or friends in on the fact that there was an affair. This is often a hard sell to many unfaithful spouses, as most want to hide their mistakes. But having many eyes on your behavior is a terrific deterrent. We would all be much more caring and much less selfish if everything we did was known publicly. In addition, it helps the betrayed spouse share accountability with others.

As I will explain later in more detail, exposure of an affair is not only an important extraordinary precaution to avoid another affair, but it's also one of the quickest ways to end an ongoing affair. A betrayed spouse is often tempted to keep the knowledge of the affair secret, in the hope that the unfaithful spouse will appreciate the enabling gesture. But as most people who help addicts know, keeping their addiction a secret only makes matters worse.

Exposure of an ongoing affair usually makes the unfaithful spouse very upset. Threats of ending the marriage are common. But we've found that when exposure doesn't end the affair, nothing else would have ended it either. In almost all cases, the light of day that exposure creates ends the illusion and helps lift the fog in the mind of the unfaithful spouse.

By letting his boss, children, friends, and relatives know about his affair, Kevin was able to explain honestly why he had to change his job location and take some of the other precautions. His honesty and openness helped him gain support for these changes.

Are Extraordinary Precautions Necessary When There Is Less Emotional Attachment?

The deep emotional attachment of soul-mate affairs makes them so difficult to end that these eight extraordinary precautions usually seem reasonable, especially to a betrayed spouse. When these measures are taken, a relapse is very unusual.

But what about affairs with less emotional attachment? And what about one-night stands? Is it really necessary to follow these guidelines in these situations?

I recommend these extraordinary precautions for all types of affairs, even one-night stands, for two reasons. First, any contact an unfaithful spouse has with a former lover is an offense to a betrayed spouse. Once a sexual relationship has occurred, or even threatens to occur, further contact should be eliminated out of consideration to the spouse.

My second reason is that it's difficult to judge the degree of attachment between the lovers in affairs, so precautions must be taken just in case the attachment is greater than the unfaithful spouse admits. They will often argue that they have no emotional feelings toward the lover as a ploy to try to continue the relationship. If there really is no attachment, then the extraordinary precautions I recommend will simply be easier to implement. But if there is resistance, it may reflect a significant attachment.

I believe that the extraordinary precautions I recommend do more than help couples end marriage-threatening affairs—they also help a couple form the kind of relationship they always wanted. And that's the best reason to use my extraordinary precautions for separating an unfaithful spouse from a lover—they not only help separate them, but they also help create a strong marriage. These conditions are not a punishment for unfaithfulness; they are crucial building blocks that form the foundation for a strong marital recovery.

> *These extraordinary precautions do more than end marriage-threatening affairs; they help a couple form the kind of relationship they always wanted.*

These recommendations may seem rigid, unnecessarily confining, and even paranoid to those who have not been the victim of infidelity. But people like Sue and Jon, who have suffered unimaginable pain as a result of an affair that spun out of control, can easily see their value. For the inconvenience of following my advice, Sue would have spared herself and Jon the very worst experience of their lives.

Checklist for How Affairs Should End

___ The unfaithful spouse should reveal information about the affair to the betrayed spouse.

___ The unfaithful spouse should make a commitment to the betrayed spouse to never see or talk to the lover again.

___ The unfaithful spouse should write a letter to the lover ending the relationship and send it with the approval of the betrayed spouse.

___ The unfaithful spouse should take extraordinary precautions to guarantee total separation from the lover:

    ___ Block potential communication with the lover (change email address and home and cell phone numbers, and close all internet social networking accounts; have voice messages and mail monitored by the betrayed spouse).

    ___ Account for time (betrayed spouse and unfaithful spouse give each other a twenty-four-hour daily schedule with locations and phone numbers).

    ___ Account for money (betrayed spouse and unfaithful spouse give each other a complete account of all money spent).

    ___ Spend leisure time together.

    ___ Change jobs and relocate, if necessary.

    ___ Avoid overnight separation.

    ___ Allow technical accountability.

    ___ Expose the affair to family members, clergy, and/or friends.

6

What to Do if the Unfaithful Spouse Continues to Contact the Lover

Sue had made a genuine effort to avoid seeing Greg—for about a week. But then she broke down and contacted him and secretly reestablished her relationship with him. As part of her deception, she tried to make Jon think she was avoiding contact.

But it soon became apparent to Sue that she couldn't live with Jon and still see Greg as often as she wanted. So she moved out with the excuse that she needed time to think. Away from Jon and on her own, she was free to be with Greg without any interference or explanation.

Most affairs do not end with a willingness to end all contact with the lover. They continue on after they are first discovered.

You may think that after a spouse willfully chooses a lover and abandons the family, as Sue did, there would be no hope for marital reconciliation, but that's not true. While there is no hope for reconciliation when the affair is underway, as soon as the affair is ended reconciliation is definitely possible. And almost all affairs end sooner than most people think they will.

But for the betrayed spouse, the wait for the affair to end seems like an eternity. The unfaithful spouse can't seem to make up his or her mind—one moment committing to the marriage and the next moment committing to the lover. To help a betrayed spouse survive that painful period of vacillation when the unfaithful spouse is continuing to contact the lover, I recommend a two-plan strategy.

The first (plan A) is designed to help the unfaithful spouse end the affair the right way—break off contact completely. If it is unsuccessful, the second plan (plan B) helps keep the marriage together until all contact with the lover has ended. This sequence, plan A followed by plan B, represents the most sensible approach to handling an unfaithful spouse's inability to decide between the lover and the betrayed spouse.

Plan A: Expose the Affair and Express a Sincere Willingness to Resolve Marital Problems

One of the quickest ways to end an affair is to expose it to the light of day. Reality has a way of bursting the bubble of illusion, and an affair is one of the biggest illusions that anyone can experience in life. It's based almost entirely on emotions with almost no logic to support it.

That fact becomes clear when children, employers, clergy, family, and friends all hear about the affair. Because they are not in the fog, they see the affair for what it really is: the cruelest, most devastating, and selfish act anyone can ever inflict on a spouse. With so many people seeing the situation logically and not emotionally, the unfaithful spouse has an opportunity to be advised and influenced by these people. Furthermore, the betrayed spouse gains support when he or she needs it the most.

I also encourage the betrayed spouse to expose the affair to the other person's spouse and sometimes their entire family. It should not be done in a spirit of anger or revenge, but rather with compassion toward those who find themselves similarly threatened by the affair.

As you can well imagine, the betrayed spouse is usually very reluctant to expose the affair when it's first discovered. He or she is often afraid that it will end the marriage. In fact, unfaithful spouses will often threaten to divorce if anyone is told about the affair.

But my experience with the thousands of couples who do expose the affair has proven to me that the risk is well worth taking. Scores of unfaithful spouses have testified to me that without exposure, their affair would have persisted indefinitely, significantly raising the risk of divorce. Exposure makes divorce less likely, not more likely.

Are There Exceptions to Immediately Exposing an Affair?

It's been my experience that the advantages of immediate exposure usually far outweigh the disadvantages. But there are a few situations where I would not suggest immediately exposing an affair.

PHYSICAL VIOLENCE

In every instance of physical violence in marriage, I have recommended separation along with a restraining order to prevent any contact between spouses. No one who has followed my advice under my direct supervision has ever experienced injury in my thirty-five years of counseling tens of thousands of couples. And I have counseled some very violent spouses.

If a wife tells me that her husband has a history of physical violence toward her, and she's discovered his affair, I suggest that she make immediate plans for a complete separation. Generally, I refer her to a shelter for abused women. After the separation is complete and she is safe, I then recommend exposure of the affair. Plan A is ruled out, and plan B, which I'll describe in the next section, is followed (no contact between spouses). Contact is restored only after the violent spouse has enrolled in an anger management program, has no contact with the lover, and is willing to begin a program of marital reconciliation.

UNCERTAINTY REGARDING THE AFFAIR

Many of the cases I've witnessed involve suspected affairs with no firm proof. In those situations, I do not recommend exposure. Instead, I suggest gathering evidence that would convince a jury that an affair has taken place. In some cases I suggest hiring an investigator to gather that evidence. Once there is certainty regarding the affair, I then recommend immediate exposure.

Affairs are not usually difficult to prove. That's because an affair is an addiction, and addicts are notoriously sloppy in covering their tracks. They also become progressively more sloppy as the affair develops. They try to hide it, and are reasonably successful early in a relationship. But eventually they leave text messages, email, and telephone records in plain sight for anyone to observe. If a suspecting spouse is patient, it doesn't take too long or require too much effort to prove that an affair is taking place.

On the other hand, a diligent hunt for evidence may prove that the spouse hasn't been unfaithful after all. One of the best ways to learn to trust a spouse is to investigate and then find that the spouse has been trustworthy.

Those who guard their privacy in marriage, claiming that a spouse has no right to passwords, internet viewing history, email records, cell phone records, credit card accounts, and other sources of evidence, are more likely to have affairs. Privacy between spouses should never be tolerated for a host of reasons. But one of the most important reasons is that privacy, and the secret second life that it helps create, breeds infidelity. Transparency, on the other hand, is one of the most important safeguards of marriage.

ECONOMIC CONSIDERATIONS

Divorce, and even separation, can have dire economic consequences for a betrayed spouse. Many wives of unfaithful husbands that I've counseled are economically dependent on his income. If she exposes the affair, she fears that he will leave her, creating financial hardship. So in those cases, I generally encourage her to plan for that possibility before exposing the affair.

Women's shelters usually offer both legal and financial advice for women who find themselves dependent on irresponsible men. Temporary aid from government, religious, and other charitable agencies can provide a safety net for these women. While exposure usually causes the affair to end, these betrayed women can expose their spouse's affair with less fear when they know that separation will not leave them destitute.

When there is an affair in the workplace, my general advice is that the unfaithful spouse must quit their job and find another to avoid ever seeing or talking to the lover again. But while the affair is taking place and the unfaithful spouse is unwilling to resign, should a betrayed spouse expose the affair to the employer?

While I unhesitatingly recommend exposing the affair to friends, family, clergy, children, and the lover's spouse, I'm not so quick to suggest exposing it to an employer. That's because such exposure could have unintended legal and economic consequences. For example, the affair might constitute grounds for a sexual harassment claim by the unfaithful spouse's lover. Or it might trigger an outright firing of the spouse, making it far more difficult for them to find another job. So in these cases I usually advise the betrayed spouse to warn the unfaithful spouse that he or she will expose the affair to the employer in a month if the unfaithful spouse is still working there, giving him or her time to make a graceful exit from that job to another. Even if a new job cannot be found in a month, I recommend waiting no longer to inform the employer, unless the unfaithful spouse has already resigned.

OTHER ISSUES

Many betrayed spouses are afraid that exposure will drive the unfaithful spouse further away. While it's true that unfaithful spouses usually feel betrayed and angry when their affair is exposed, I regard that reaction as being part of the fog that most addicts experience. When the fog has finally lifted, and the source of addiction no longer has control, the value of exposure is usually conceded by the addict.

As is the case in all instances of addiction, it's tempting for a caregiver to enable the addict to continue their addiction by failing to expose their self-defeating behavior. And yet most therapists who treat addicts agree that the fastest way to help an addict recover is to expose their addiction. And, without a doubt, an affair is an addiction. You do the addict no favors by helping him or her keep it a secret. You become a partner in a deception that prolongs your agony and the agony of the addict.

Some feel that an affair should not be exposed to children. Granted, I would not tell a three-year-old about an affair, simply because a child that young cannot possibly understand what it means. But I would not hesitate to reveal an affair to a child age seven or older. Exposure to children between those ages should be a matter of discretion.

What about exposure of an affair that took place years earlier and is now ended but recently revealed? I feel that children, close relatives, close friends, and the lover's spouse should be informed. Granted, it's embarrassing to admit an affair, but publicly admitting failure is usually the first step toward redemption.

As you probably already know, I'm a strong advocate of honesty and openness in marriage. But should that level of openness carry into the public arena? I believe that it should in cases of extreme irresponsibility, and that certainly includes infidelity. When you have done something very hurtful to someone else, others should know about it. Such exposure helps prevent a recurrence of the offense. Your closest friends and relatives will be keeping an eye on you, holding you accountable.

If exposure of an affair threatens the marriage, should the risk be taken? I regard infidelity as a violation of the most basic condition of marriage. In most wedding vows, "forsaking all others" is usually the only definitive promise that's made. When you marry, the overriding condition that is mutually accepted is that you won't have an affair. When that condition is broken, the marriage is threatened at its very core. That's why I believe spouses who have recovered after an affair should make new vows to each other, in effect reestablishing their marriage.

So when a betrayed spouse asks for my advice, I usually take the position that infidelity is the greatest betrayal of all. After an affair, trust, which is an essential ingredient in marriage, is dashed. If the unfaithful spouse is offended by being exposed, so be it. Exposure is very likely to end the affair, lifting the fog that has overcome the unfaithful spouse, helping him or her become truly repentant and willing to put energy and effort into a full marital recovery.

In my experience with thousands of couples who struggle with the fallout of infidelity, exposure has been the single most important first step toward recovery. It not only helps end the affair, but it also provides support to the betrayed spouse, giving him or her stamina to hold out for ultimate marital recovery.

But There's More to Plan A than Exposure

Plan A involves much more than just exposing the affair: it also sends a clear message that the betrayed spouse will help to resolve marital problems that may have contributed to the affair. When the betrayed spouse makes a commitment to follow the plan of recovery that I recommend after the affair is over, the complaints of the unfaithful spouse are taken seriously.

In most cases, when an unfaithful spouse's affair is discovered, they see their choice as either living in a loveless, unfulfilling marriage or enjoying a love-filled relationship that the affair provides. The commitment of the betrayed spouse to help create a love-filled marriage provides hope for a third alternative—a fulfilling marriage.

As mentioned previously, while there are no excuses for an affair, there are usually reasons that create the vulnerability. And one of the most common reasons is that important emotional needs are not being met in the marriage. Plan A addresses that issue, which makes it easier for the unfaithful spouse to end the affair.

Exposure is difficult enough for the betrayed spouse. But making a sincere commitment to help resolve marital conflicts after the affair is over can be even more difficult. A betrayed spouse isn't even sure that he or she wants the marriage to continue after an affair. Anger and disrespect toward the unfaithful spouse are very common. Yet, if plan A is to be followed, they must be completely eliminated.

If a betrayed spouse has difficulty editing out disrespectful and angry comments when conversing with their unfaithful spouse, I will often suggest communicating through email and phone calls. In an email, a betrayed spouse is able to choose words carefully and a phone call allows both spouses to end the call if it becomes abusive.

In many cases, an unfaithful spouse makes no effort to encourage the betrayed spouse. They act in ways that demonstrate blatant disregard for the betrayed spouse's feelings. Plan A is an attempt to help an unfaithful spouse end an affair, but if the affair persists, how long can a betrayed spouse endure the suffering that it causes? With that suffering in mind, I suggest a time limit for plan A. Quite frankly, there's a limit to everyone's patience.

For most women I recommend about a three-week limit for plan A, because my experience has taught me that the health of wives tends to deteriorate quickly and significantly when living with an unfaithful husband. For most men, on the other hand, I recommend a much longer effort: at least six months. I've found that husbands tend to be able to weather the storm with fewer emotional and physical effects. But once plan A ends, plan B should immediately take its place.

Plan B: Avoid All Contact with the Unfaithful Spouse until the Affair Has Ended

The primary objective of plan B is to protect the betrayed spouse from the severe physical and emotional effects of the unfaithful spouse's affair. By avoiding all contact, the stress of the affair is reduced considerably, and the betrayed spouse is able to feel much better and think more clearly. If contact continues, the stress can lead to physical and emotional problems that persist long after the affair is over and the marriage is restored.

But there are two other important reasons for plan B. One is to preserve the betrayed spouse's love for the unfaithful spouse, and the other is to give the unfaithful spouse a taste of what it's like to live without the betrayed spouse.

An affair can take quite a toll on a betrayed spouse's Love Bank. It's the most painful experience a spouse can ever endure, and it can cause major Love Bank withdrawals. Ordinarily, I encourage couples to spend as much time together as possible, because that gives them opportunity to meet each other's emotional needs. But while one spouse is having an affair, all bets are off. Emotional needs cannot be met effectively and thoughtlessness runs rampant. Love Bank withdrawals far outweigh deposits. So by avoiding all contact with the unfaithful spouse, a betrayed spouse is able to preserve the deposits that remain in his or her Love Bank.

Avoiding all contact also lets both spouses know how they will be affected by divorce. For the betrayed spouse, it's an opportunity to look to the future without the burden of the unfaithful spouse. With the suffering that he or she caused by the affair, avoiding contact can be a great relief that opens opportunities for a new and attractive way of life.

But with plan A just passed, with the betrayed spouse having presented an attractive proposal to meet the unfaithful spouse's emotional needs and avoid being a source of unhappiness when they reconcile, the unfaithful spouse has an opportunity to reflect on what he or she will be missing with a divorce.

In most affairs, the betrayed spouse meets some of the unfaithful spouse's emotional needs and the lover meets other needs. When Sue and Jon were living together, and she was having the affair with Greg, she had the best of both worlds. With Greg she had intimate conversation, affection, and recreational companionship, and with Jon she had his financial support and family commitment. Her affair was an uncomfortable juggling act for Sue, but her needs were being met. If Jon had not asked so many questions and made it so difficult for Sue to sneak off to be with Greg, she would have let this go on indefinitely. But she was the one who finally decided to separate so that she could have easier access to Greg. Jon and Sue didn't know it at the time, but her separation actually helped her affair die a natural death.

Of course, plan B does tend to throw the unfaithful spouse into the waiting arms of the lover. So doesn't that give the affair the chance it needs to succeed?

Most affairs are based on fantasy and wishful thinking. In reality, the lover is not an improvement over the betrayed spouse, and giving an affair a chance can actually prove that it won't succeed. Love units were deposited into Greg's account in Sue's Love Bank because they were *not* together as husband and wife, battling through the tough problems of daily living. They were together only when Sue was escaping the hard realities of her otherwise unfulfilling life. By letting Greg become involved in all aspects of her life, his ability to handle her problems was put to the test. And, like most lovers when tested, Greg failed. Sue found herself feeling unfulfilled with him, too.

Keep in mind that a strong support group is needed for the betrayed spouse during a time of separation. Pleasant surroundings are also important. A betrayed spouse should try to arrange things to be reasonably comfortable. So I highly recommend careful preparation for plan B. An attorney should be consulted to be sure that the separation does not jeopardize custody or financial settlement if a divorce becomes inevitable.

Since there is to be no contact with the unfaithful spouse, the betrayed spouse should move as far away as possible. An attorney can provide advice on the legal implications of a move for the state in which the couple reside.

Plan B usually requires an arrangement with their mutual friends to handle all necessary communication so that there is no need for the betrayed spouse to see or talk to the unfaithful spouse directly unless they happen to accidentally cross paths.

An example of a letter explaining the purpose of the separation and what would be required for reconciliation is as follows:

My Dearest _____,

I apologize to you for my part in creating an environment that helped make your affair possible. I foolishly pursued my goals without understanding my responsibility to meet your most important emotional needs. I was not there for you when you needed me the most and we are now both suffering for my mistake. [Add your willingness to address other complaints that the unfaithful spouse may have communicated prior to the affair.]

I am willing to avoid the mistakes I've made in the past and create a new life for both of us that will meet your needs. But I cannot do that until you end your relationship once and for all. Living with you under these conditions has been the most painful experience of my life, and I can no longer endure it.

Until your affair ends, and you are willing to follow a plan of reconciliation with me, I will avoid seeing you or talking to you. Our friends, _____, have agreed to help make arrangements for you to see our children on a schedule that is mutually convenient. They will provide transportation. If you want to communicate about the children or any other matter, it will have to be through them.

I ask you to respect my decision to separate from you this way. You must know about the suffering I have endured because of your relationship, and I simply cannot be with you any longer knowing that you are together. I still love you but I cannot see you under these conditions.

As soon as you are willing to permanently end your relationship, follow precautions to avoid absolutely any contact with the other person, and join me in a plan to restore our relationship, I will be willing to discuss our future together with you.

I hope that we will be able to rebuild our marriage some day. I want us to be able to meet each other's emotional needs and to avoid doing anything to hurt each other. We can build a new lifestyle together in which everything we do makes us both happy. Then there will never again be a reason for us to be separated. I want to be your best friend, someone who is always there for you when you need me. And I want you as my best friend.

I cared for you when we married and I continue to care for you right up to this day. But I cannot be with you or help you as long as you are in this relationship.

With all my love,
(signed)

This letter should be delivered by your friends to the unfaithful spouse, and a copy sent to the lover with a note at the bottom saying:

I love _____ with all my heart and am willing to do whatever it takes to make (him/her) happy. I will wait for that chance.

How Long Should You Wait?

How long should a betrayed spouse be separated under plan B before filing for divorce? It's been my experience that a separation lasting two years rarely leads to marital recovery. In some cases, once the affair has died a natural death, the unfaithful spouse finds another lover rather than reconciling. So just as plan A should have a time limit, I also recommend one for plan B. Two years is usually what I recommend.

One of the objectives of plan B is to help the unfaithful spouse see what they're missing. In Sue's case, when she moved to her own apartment, she missed being with her children and ran out of money to support herself. But her counselor and attorney helped her solve those problems. They advised her to file for a legal separation, return home, and kick Jon out. Shortly after returning home she obtained a court order for Jon to pay her three thousand dollars a month in child support. He was forced by law to meet her need for financial support that was not being met by Greg.

But money was not the only thing that Jon had provided Sue—he had also provided care and security for her children. While he was at home with his daughters, the girls had hoped that their mother would eventually return to them and that their family would be reunited. But when Sue did return, she forced Jon to leave his girls, something they had not anticipated. They were both very angry toward Sue for forcing him to leave. They missed their dad terribly.

Sue now had money and the comfort of her home, but her children, whom she loved dearly, were devastated. They had liked Greg, but now they disliked him because their mom was trying to replace their dad with him. It was not a happy homecoming for Sue.

Sue's affair ended just as most affairs end. In some cases, it's the wayward spouse who realizes that the other person cannot offer enough to compensate for the loss of his or her marriage. In other cases, like Sue's, it's the other person who realizes that the wayward spouse is not worth the hassle. When Greg was seeing Sue in secret, their relationship was filled with excitement and anticipation. But when it was out into the open, the problems of real life, and their inability to solve them, torpedoed the fun they had together.

Sue was depressed most of the time and there was nothing Greg could do to lift her spirits. Her girls became outwardly hostile toward him and he found his relationship with Sue increasingly difficult. No love units were being deposited into her account in his Love Bank and many were being withdrawn. Eventually there were none left. So he began a relationship with another woman who did not have children and ended his relationship with Sue. If he had not ended it, I'm sure that Sue would have eventually ended it herself.

Even so, Sue was devastated when Greg left her. She had given up almost everything to have Greg with her and now he was gone. She was left with her house, her children, and Jon's financial support. But now there was no one to meet her other emotional needs—no one, that is, but Jon.

How to Pick Up the Pieces after an Affair Dies a Natural Death

By the time Sue's affair had died a natural death and she had invited Jon to return to their home, they were both ready to begin their recovery. But when they came to me for counseling, they had both lost their love for each other.

After all that Sue had put Jon through, you'd think she would have been humbled and deeply remorseful. Sometimes an unfaithful spouse does ask for forgiveness for the incredible thoughtlessness of his or her affair, but

Sue didn't. In fact the way she talked to Jon about getting back together sounded as if he was the one who had had the affair. She made it seem as if he was lucky to have another chance to win her back.

A betrayed spouse usually expects their unfaithful spouse to express guilt and remorse over the pain inflicted by the thoughtlessness of the affair, and Jon was no exception. He felt that an apology was necessary before he would be willing to reconcile. But I was able to talk him out of this condition, because I knew that at the beginning of recovery, remorse is rarely expressed. I suggested that he avoid the subject of regret or even forgiveness. Instead, I wanted him to focus on what they both needed to do to meet each other's emotional needs and become more thoughtful of each other's feelings.

I've found that an apology is not always necessary for a full marital recovery to take place after an affair. Of course, if remorse is actually felt by a spouse, I encourage that spouse to express it. The unfaithful spouse should apologize for having betrayed a valuable trust and for having hurt in the worst way possible the very one he or she promised to love and cherish. But since I've witnessed thousands of marital recoveries when the unfaithful spouse has not offered an apology at first, I don't require it.

If the feeling of remorse is not actually felt by a spouse, I don't recommend a reluctant apology. I don't see any sense in mouthing words that don't reflect true feelings. Insincere words won't help marital recovery. It's the new lifestyle that the couple creates that will save their marriage.

If the feeling of remorse is not actually felt by a spouse, I don't recommend a reluctant apology.

Instead of focusing their attention on the mistakes of the past, I encourage couples to focus on the present and future. They should NOT dwell on the affair but focus on rebuilding their marriage. Every time the affair is mentioned, love units are withdrawn from both Love Banks. So the less time spent talking about the affair, the better. If the couple is already painfully aware of the details of the tragedy, there's no value in being reminded of what they already know.

This is not to say that the betrayed spouse shouldn't ask questions about the affair if unanswered questions remain. Radical honesty is the new lifestyle rule of a couple in recovery. So for this situation, I recommend that the betrayed spouse make a list of questions, schedule a specific day to ask them, and receive honest answers. But once the questions are answered honestly, the affair should not be mentioned again.

The goal of marital recovery is to make enough Love Bank deposits and avoid enough withdrawals for the Love Banks of both spouses to overflow. The reconciled couple must learn how to build a new lifestyle that achieves that objective, and my plan for marital recovery helps couples learn how to create that lifestyle.

Checklist for What to Do If the Unfaithful Spouse Continues to Contact the Lover

Plan A: Expose the affair and express a sincere willingness to resolve marital problems

___ Expose the affair to your children, employers, clergy, family, friends, and the lover's spouse, family, and/or friends (with exceptions as discussed regarding threat of physical violence, financial considerations, uncertainty regarding the affair, and age of children).

___ Express commitment to the unfaithful spouse to meet emotional needs, avoid being a source of unhappiness, and resolve marital conflicts that may have contributed to the affair.

___ Avoid disrespectful judgments and angry outbursts.

___ Set a time limit.

Plan B: Avoid all contact with the unfaithful spouse until the affair has ended

___ Plan the separation carefully, making sure that you will be as comfortable as possible. Seek legal advice if you have children.

___ Create an encouraging support group who will assist you.

___ Write a letter to the unfaithful spouse explaining why all contact must end and what can be done to restore it.

___ Send a copy of that letter to the lover adding an explanation that you love your spouse and want the marriage to succeed.

___ Take extraordinary measures to avoid contact with the unfaithful spouse until the affair has ended and a willingness to follow a plan of reconciliation is communicated.

___ Set a time limit.

7

The First Steps on the Road to Marital Recovery

When Kevin decided to end his relationship with Amy, he made the right decision. But he didn't make that decision just once. In the days that followed he had to make the decision many times. He was tempted to give Amy a call every day just to hear her voice, and every day he made the decision not to call her.

How long will this last? Kevin wanted to know. *I'm not sure I can do this much longer.* Only three days had passed since he had last talked to Amy, and he was already overwhelmed by the pain of being separated from her. He was just a phone call away from ending that pain—by just talking to her.

I did my best to encourage Kevin. Antidepressant medication prescribed by his doctor also helped relieve some of his most intense feelings of hopelessness. But it was Kevin's willingness to follow the extraordinary precautions that actually kept him away from Amy (see chapter 5).

An Affair Offers No Painless Escape

Kevin may have suffered after he separated from Amy. But by separating early in the affair, he spared himself, Lee, and his children untold additional suffering that they would have experienced if he had not separated from her when he did.

But Sue and Jon were not spared that additional suffering. Although Sue tried to separate from Greg after Jon discovered their affair, her failure to take extraordinary precautions to guarantee separation caused her and her family so much pain that it almost ruined their lives.

Most people who have affairs are like Sue—they don't do what it takes to make a clean break from their lover. Sue lost perspective for what was important in her life. She was willing to sacrifice her children, her reputation, and her financial security just to continue her relationship with Greg. The inability to separate makes the tragedy of an affair much more painful than it would be if the lovers separated early.

When people like Sue try to leave their lover and experience the pain of withdrawal, they often cannot resist the temptation to return to the affair. But returning to the lover does not alleviate their depression for long. In fact for many, the momentary emotional relief after reconciliation with the lover is followed by depression returning with a vengeance. After going back to the lover, it doesn't usually take long before the unfaithful spouse feels so depressed that suicide is often considered to be the only escape. They cannot imagine leaving their lover, nor can they imagine leaving their family. They see no hope. They know they are causing their spouse and children unbearable pain, yet they seem powerless to stop the affair.

Sue told me, *I knew what I was doing was stupid. I was going to lose everything but I just couldn't leave Greg. I couldn't choose between Greg and my family.* She had lost almost everything to stay with Greg just a little longer. It took Greg's decision to leave her to end her addiction to him. But by the time his decision was made, she felt some relief. At last the trap was opened and she was free. But when she returned to Jon, she still missed Greg.

Without a doubt, Sue suffered far more than Kevin because she didn't end her affair the right way. She let her affair drag on, keeping her in an almost continual state of depression. But when her affair had finally died a natural death, and she had returned to her husband, she still suffered the symptoms of withdrawal. She still had feelings for Greg when I began to help her on the road to marital recovery.

Granted, it was easier for her to put the affair behind her, since it was Greg who ended it. He refused to talk with her after they broke up. But both Sue and Kevin faced the emotional effects of withdrawal—being separated from the source of their addiction.

Getting through Withdrawal

Kevin was going through an experience that those familiar with addiction know all too well—withdrawal—the emotional reaction a person experiences when separated from the object of his or her addiction.

The feelings of withdrawal and grief are very similar. They are both emotional reactions that are associated with the loss of a very valuable part of one's life, something that provided great pleasure and satisfaction. In the case of grief, the loss is usually final—loss of a home by fire or a loved one by death. However, in the case of withdrawal, whether from alcohol or a lover, the loss doesn't have to be final. All that's needed to recover the loss is to return to the object of addiction. And that's why Kevin was faced with hundreds of decisions to leave Amy—he could have her back any time he wanted.

During the first few weeks after total separation from a lover, the depression that accompanies the loss can be so pervasive and overwhelming that nothing makes the wayward spouse happy. That was certainly Kevin's experience. There was no escape from the loss that he felt. He simply had to get through the withdrawal period before he could enjoy his life again.

Lee wanted to quickly straighten out whatever had been missing in her marriage. That's what many spouses do when they get over the shock of discovering that their spouse was unfaithful. If it was sex that was missing, the spouse wants to offer more and better sex. If it was affection, it's more and better affection. If it was conversation, more and better conversation. A spouse is often willing to do almost anything to regain a wayward spouse's love. But these initial efforts to meet the unfaithful spouse's emotional needs are usually disappointing during the first few weeks of withdrawal because he or she is so unhappy.

I warned Lee that her efforts to cheer Kevin up might seem to her as wasted effort during the first few weeks of his separation from Amy.

However, by applying those extraordinary precautions I had recommended, the symptoms of withdrawal would begin to fade. And as they faded, Lee and Kevin would become increasingly effective in depositing love units into each other's Love Banks.

The Symptoms of Withdrawal

Someone going through withdrawal usually experiences depression, anxiety, and anger—all in a very intense form. The feeling of utter hopelessness, the fear of making a catastrophic mistake, and even anger toward a betrayed spouse are often overwhelming. These reactions are usually so severe that I often suggest that the wayward spouse consult with his or her doctor for antidepressant medication to help stabilize these symptoms during this most unpleasant experience.

But if there is total separation from the lover, the most intense symptoms of withdrawal usually last only about three weeks and then fade almost entirely over the next six months. But if a slip occurs and contact is made with a lover during withdrawal, the clock goes back to zero, and the period of withdrawal starts all over again. So I've found that those few who report lingering withdrawal symptoms after six months are usually guilty of making sporadic contact with the former lover and lying about that contact to their spouse.

Lee was concerned about Kevin's depression. She had never seen him react this way before. I had warned both of them that the symptoms of withdrawal were almost inevitable, but the warning did not prepare her for the extreme form they took. At first, Kevin experienced a total loss of energy and could hardly face each day. In reality, events were turning out to his advantage, but through the fog of his depression, he couldn't see anything but doom and gloom. For example, even though his boss was very understanding and cooperative, offering him a job at another dealership, Kevin came away feeling as though the meeting had been a disaster.

Kevin was spending all of his nonworking hours with Lee and his children—these were my instructions—but Kevin's depression rubbed off on Lee and made her feel depressed, too. After a few days, neither of them were sure it was a good idea to be together.

They were in a temporary, but very necessary, holding pattern during which their relationship wasn't improving much. Kevin's symptoms of withdrawal had to fade significantly before his marital recovery could get completely on track. But being together was still an important step in the recovery process. They had to be together to prevent Kevin's return to Amy; and even though their efforts were disappointing, a few love units managed to get through.

I instructed them to completely avoid demands, disrespect, and anger while they were together. I also encouraged them to try to be affectionate and make love to each other. But their primary goal was to simply keep each other company for a few weeks and avoid doing anything that would make matters worse. Opportunities to meet each other's emotional needs more effectively would come later.

The exercise that Lee was getting three mornings a week with Kevin helped keep her emotionally stable. The assurances I gave her also helped keep her in a positive mood. The time it takes for withdrawal to end seems like an eternity when it is taking place, but the worst is usually over in about a month. I kept reminding Lee of that fact.

Kevin and Lee followed my suggestions to ensure separation from Amy. Kevin gave Lee a schedule of his daily activities, and she gave him hers. They exercised together and called each other during the day, and Kevin spent as much time as possible with Lee.

Some of the best examples of recovery I've witnessed involved couples who were forced, due to a prior business or vacation commitment, to be together almost twenty-four hours a day for about a month during withdrawal. It's the perfect formula for withdrawal because it helps ensure total separation from a lover.

Most couples, however, are not fortunate enough to have such advantageous preplanning. So I often recommend an extended vacation or successive weekend getaways for a couple going through withdrawal. The wayward spouse's depression is often so severe that getting away from everything can provide a welcome relief.

Granted, for the betrayed spouse, taking a vacation after such trauma may, at first, seem like "sleeping with the enemy." But it provides a great opportunity to be together in a comfortable setting that minimizes the withdrawal of love units and maximizes deposits.

The extraordinary precautions worked for Kevin and Lee. Kevin did not talk to Amy again, and the intense emotional reaction he experienced initially faded within a few weeks.

Beginning at Different Places on the Road to Recovery

Sue's affair with Greg and Kevin's affair with Amy were strikingly similar. They both began as a friendship and they both developed into a love relationship because important emotional needs had been met. By learning to meet each other's needs, Sue and Greg and Kevin and Amy had fallen in love.

But there was one very important difference in these affairs. Sue's affair with Greg became sexual, while Kevin's never got that far. As soon as Kevin and Amy expressed their love for each other, Kevin realized that he was in trouble. He wisely confessed his feelings to Lee and ended his relationship with Amy.

Some would argue that Kevin never really had an affair, because they feel that a relationship outside marriage must be sexual to be considered an affair. But an emotional affair can be even more of a threat to marriage than a sexual affair. And unless Kevin had separated from Amy when he did, they would have eventually made love. I believe that anyone who is in love with someone outside of marriage, and expresses that love to him or her, is having an affair. This is particularly true when that expression of love is reciprocated.

In spite of this important difference between the two affairs—one was sexual while the other was not—my plan for marital recovery was the same for both of them. Its purpose is to rebuild Love Bank accounts and keep those accounts healthy. It's a plan to create a new lifestyle that helps a couple maintain mutual love and compatibility. It also protects a couple from a new affair.

But while the plan was the same for both couples, they began at different places on the road to recovery. Sue's affair had withdrawn so many love units from her account in Jon's Love Bank that by the time they reunited it was deeply in the red—she had a negative balance. Jon had not just stopped loving her, he had started *disliking* her. And Jon's account in Sue's Love Bank wasn't in much better shape. Although he had tried to meet her emotional needs while she was having her affair, her love for Greg prevented Jon's care from reaching her, so none of it was recorded in her Love Bank.

Kevin and Lee, on the other hand, began their recovery with Love Bank accounts that had not taken much of a beating. The discovery of the affair was hard on Kevin's account in Lee's Love Bank, but the damage was minimized by the way he handled it—totally separating from Amy. So it was not only easier for them to follow my plan for recovery, but they saw positive results more quickly.

> *An emotional affair can be even more of a threat to marriage than a sexual affair.*

Since Sue and Jon had the harder and longer road to recovery, I will focus on their experience trying to follow my plan. Their reconciliation was more difficult because Sue's affair had not ended the right way—with immediate total separation from Greg after she realized she was in love with him. By pursuing the affair, Sue created many emotional obstacles to recovery. But my plan is designed to overcome even these obstacles.

By the time Sue's affair was over, and Greg had refused to talk with her, she was willing to reconcile for the sake of her girls—and herself. Her daughters wanted their dad back, and with Greg out of the picture, there was no reason to keep Jon from them. Besides, she longed to return to the days when her life was normal. Maybe having Jon home would turn the clock back to those happier days, even if she no longer felt love for Jon and had little hope of ever loving him the way she loved Greg.

Jon wasn't all that enthusiastic about reconciliation. He felt like he had been through a war and didn't think he could ever trust Sue again. Jon had spent quite a bit of time planning for this very day, the day he would return to Sue, but he didn't feel like celebrating. He was, however, ready and willing to follow my plan for recovery.

Build Love Bank Balances: Make Deposits and Avoid Withdrawals

My plan for recovery after an affair is very logical. If a couple wants their marriage to recover, they must restore their feeling of love for each other. And that restoration of love requires them to build their Love Bank balances, making large Love Bank deposits and avoiding withdrawals. If they make enough deposits to breach the romantic love threshold, they will restore their feeling of love for each other. It's that simple.

But after an affair, it isn't so simple to make the necessary deposits while avoiding the withdrawals. In fact, most spouses who have just experienced the tragedy of an affair *feel* like doing the opposite—making more withdrawals and avoiding deposits.

So the plan I recommend is logical, but counterintuitive. Most people know that it's the right thing to do, yet they don't feel like doing it. It may sound like an impossible assignment when Love Bank balances are in the red, but I've witnessed thousands of couples who have successfully followed this program of recovery to its completion. I know it can be done!

There are two basic parts to my program of recovery. The first part is to learn how to make each other very happy—to make massive Love Bank deposits. Even a couple like Sue and Jon, who began the program with negative Love Bank balances, can begin the process of recovery by meeting each other's most important emotional needs. But there's no point in making Love Bank deposits if a couple continue to make withdrawals. So the second basic part of my program of recovery is to learn to avoid what I call Love Busters—habits that make your spouse unhappy. I focus a couple's attention on six Love Busters, each one capable of making massive Love Bank withdrawals.

When a couple first come to me for help, I would like to be able to instantly give them the ability to meet each other's emotional needs and to avoid Love Busters. They are so damaged by the affair that they can't afford to make additional mistakes. But it takes time to achieve these crucial objectives. So I prioritize which one of these two objectives is causing the greatest obstacle to their recovery, and begin by trying to achieve that one first.

While helping a couple with their most crucial objective at first, I don't ignore the other one. I begin their recovery with a general summary of both essential objectives so that they can understand the value in achieving them all. In many cases, once the biggest obstacle is overcome, the couple can overcome the other without much help.

Where to Begin

When Jon and Sue first counseled with me, I discovered what they needed most by asking them to complete several forms. First I familiarized them with the ten emotional needs (appendix A) and then they completed the Emotional Needs Questionnaire (appendix B). This helped them understand what they could do for each other that would make the most Love Bank deposits.

The second form I asked them to complete was the Love Busters Questionnaire (appendix C). It identified how they'd been making massive Love Bank withdrawals, and how they could avoid doing it. The third form was the Memorandum of Agreement (appendix D). This agreement summarized the emotional needs that they should meet for each other and the Love Busters they should avoid. When they signed that agreement, their recovery had begun.

In the case of Jon and Sue, the primary reason for Sue's vulnerability to have an affair was that Jon was too busy at work to meet her emotional needs. It created a void that was filled by Greg. So you'd think that their plan for recovery would begin by teaching Jon to meet Sue's emotional needs. But when Love Bank balances are in the red, a couple tends to hurt each other almost instinctively. So in their case, and for most other couples I counsel, their recovery began with the elimination of Love Busters.

Your case may be different, however. So to make your plan fit your situation, I encourage you to use these forms to help you decide where to start. Should you try to overcome Love Busters first, or tackle unmet emotional needs first? If you don't agree where to begin, I suggest that you do what Jon and Sue did—eliminate Love Busters first. It makes sense, because if either of you feels attacked by the other person's Love Busters, you won't make much progress trying to meet each other's emotional needs.

In the following chapters, I will explain in detail how to complete the three forms and implement the two parts to my program of marital recovery after an affair. So I suggest that you read the remainder of this book in its entirety before you finalize your plan.

8

Avoid Withdrawals, Part I

Overcome Love Busters

*M*y ultimate goal for Jon and Sue was the restoration of their love for each other. To achieve that goal, they had to redeposit all of the love units that had been withdrawn over the past two years—and then deposit even more. But before I would focus their attention on depositing those love units, I had to be sure they would avoid withdrawing them.

Knowing that his wife was having an affair was the most painful experience of Jon's life, and when it was over he had very little compassion for Sue. He wanted to have an affair himself so she would know how it felt. He wanted to lecture her on how thoughtless she had been. He wanted to remind her of the pain he had endured. He wanted to punish her just to even the score.

Fortunately I was able to convince Jon that those instinctive responses would eventually drive Sue away from him again and make the chances of their marital recovery very unlikely. If he really wanted to save his marriage, he had to protect Sue from his negative emotional reactions—at all costs.

Even though Sue was the one who had the affair, she was also angry and resentful toward Jon. She did not welcome him home with remorse for what she had put him through. Instead, she felt that the whole ordeal was all his fault. If Jon had been looking for an apology, he came to the wrong place. Sue never did apologize.

But Sue was not only unrepentant, she was also tempted to take out her anger on Jon. She had lost the one she had regarded as her soul mate for life and she somehow blamed Jon for it. Unless she would be able to protect Jon from her feelings of anger, their marital recovery would end almost as quickly as it had begun.

Jon and Sue's emotional instincts were telling them to freely express their anger and disrespect to each other. Their instincts were also encouraging them to make their decisions without considering each other's feelings. They were both hurt deeply by the events of the past two years and were very tempted to do whatever they could to make themselves feel better, even if it was at the other's expense.

If Jon and Sue were to follow the advice of their instincts, there would be no hope for marital recovery because they would be continually hurting each other. Love units would be withdrawn faster than they could ever be deposited. That's why Sue and Jon had to make a special effort to stop doing anything to hurt each other. If they didn't, whatever they would try to do to make the other happy would be wasted effort.

Love Busters: Habits That Destroy Romantic Love

Whenever you do something that makes your spouse unhappy, you make a Love Bank withdrawal. But let's face it, it's impossible to avoid all the bumps and bruises of life, especially marital bumps and bruises. Even in the best marriages, spouses hurt each other now and then.

But occasional mistakes do not drain a Love Bank as long as they're seen as mistakes. An apology usually heals the wound.

It's when a mistake turns into a habit, repeated again and again, that Love Bank balances are at great risk. In these situations, apologies mean very little because the same mistake keeps being repeated. Nothing is done to keep love units from flowing out of the Love Bank. I call these habits that drain the Love Bank "Love Busters," because they do more to ruin romantic love than anything else.

Throughout years of marriage counseling, I've been made aware of a host of Love Busters that all fall into six categories: selfish demands, disrespectful judgments, angry outbursts, annoying habits, dishonesty, and independent behavior. Because all of the categories are so important, I will discuss each of them in this chapter. Then, in the next two chapters, I'll focus special attention on dishonesty and independent behavior. These two Love Busters help create the secret second life that makes affairs possible.

Selfish Demands: Attempts to force the other to do something with implied threat of punishment if he or she refuses.

When Jon returned to Sue, he really didn't feel like doing much for her. He felt she should repay him for everything she'd put him through. But Sue didn't feel like doing much for Jon, either. With both of them feeling that the other person had lots of making up to do, they were both tempted to make demands of each other. I warned them that demands were a Love Buster, and if they tried being demanding, they would have a much more difficult time restoring love to their marriage.

Our parents made demands on us when we were children, teachers made demands on us in school, and employers make demands at work. Most of us didn't like them as children—and we still don't.

Demands carry a threat of punishment. *If you refuse me, you'll regret it.* In other words, you may dislike doing what I want, but if you don't do it, I'll see to it that you suffer even greater pain.

People who make demands don't seem to care how others feel. They think only of their own needs. *If you find it unpleasant to do what I want, tough! And if you refuse, I'll make it even tougher.*

Demands depend on power. They don't work unless the demanding one has the power to make good on the threats. But in a marriage there should be shared power: the husband and wife working together to accomplish mutual objectives with mutual agreement. When one spouse starts making demands—along with threats that are at least implied—power is no longer shared. As a result, the threatened spouse often strikes back, fighting fire with fire, power with power. Suddenly the marriage is a tug-of-war instead of a bicycle built for two. It's a test of strength—who has enough power to win? When one spouse wins and the other loses, the marriage loses.

When one spouse wins and the other loses, the marriage loses.

Demands are the wrong way to get what you need from each other. When you ask your spouse to do something for you, he or she may cheerfully agree to do it or may express reluctance. This reluctance may be due to any number of causes—personal needs, comfort level, a sense of what's wise or fair. But be assured that there is a reason for reluctance, and from your spouse's viewpoint, it's a good reason.

If you insist on your request after your spouse expresses reluctance, you turn it into a demand. You are declaring that your wishes are more important than his or her feelings. And you are threatening a distressful outcome if your demands are not met.

Now your spouse must choose the lesser of the two evils—your "punishment" on the one hand or his or her cause for reluctance on the other. Your spouse may ultimately submit to your demand, and you get your way—but it will be at your spouse's expense. I guarantee your spouse will feel used, and rightfully so. And you will withdraw love units in the process.

Sometimes a wife says, *But you don't know my husband! He lies around the house all night, and I can't get him to do a thing. The only time he lifts a finger is to press the remote control. If I don't demand that he get up and help me, nothing will get done.*

Requests don't work with my wife, a husband might say. *She only thinks about herself! She spends her whole life shopping and going out with her girlfriends. If I didn't demand that she stay at home once in a while, I'd never see her.*

My answer is that demands are an ineffective way to get a husband to help around the house or to keep a wife from going out with her friends. Demands do not encourage people to cooperate, they only withdraw love units. If you force your spouse to meet your needs, it becomes a temporary solution at best, and resentment is sure to rear its ugly head. Threats, lectures, and other forms of manipulation do not build compatibility—they build resentment.

I want to help you get everything you need from each other in your marriage. But let me make myself clear: demands never work. Not only will demands fail to get you what you need but they will make massive withdrawals from your Love Banks. A thoughtful request, asking for what you need with a willingness to consider the other person's feelings, is the only effective alternative.

Disrespectful Judgments: Attempts to change the other's attitudes, beliefs, and behavior by trying to force your way of thinking through lecture, ridicule, threat, or other means.

Jon had difficulty being respectful to Sue after what she'd put him through. It was all he could do to avoid lecturing her on the consequences of her shortsighted and thoughtless ways. After all, her life was in ruins after the affair was over. If Jon had not graciously come back to her to give their marriage another chance, it would have remained in ruins. Jon wanted to be sure that Sue had learned a lesson from it all.

But Sue didn't feel she had much to learn at all. She felt that it was Jon who had lessons to learn, and no amount of lecturing on his part would have changed her mind. It would have only infuriated her.

Have you ever tried to "straighten out" someone? We're all occasionally tempted to do it. We usually think we're doing that person a big favor, lifting him or her from the darkness of confusion into the light of our superior perspective. If people would only follow our advice, we assume, they could avoid many of life's pitfalls.

But if you ever try to straighten out your spouse, to keep him or her from making mistakes, you are making a much bigger mistake. I call it a disrespectful judgment, and your disrespectful judgment withdraws love units, destroying love.

A disrespectful judgment occurs whenever someone tries to impose a system of values and beliefs on someone else. When a husband tries to force his point of view on his wife, he's just asking for trouble. When a wife assumes that her own views are right and her husband is woefully misguided—and tells him so—she enters a minefield.

Trouble starts when you think you have the right—even the responsibility—to force your spouse to accept your point of view. Almost invariably, he or she will regard such an imposition as personally threatening, arrogant, rude, and incredibly disrespectful. That's when you lose love units in your spouse's Love Bank.

When you try to impose your opinions on your spouse, you imply that he or she has poor judgment. That's disrespectful. You may not say this in so many words, but it's the clear message that your spouse hears. If you value your spouse's judgment, you won't be so quick to discard his or her opinions. You will consider the possibility that your spouse may be right and you wrong.

I'm not saying that you can't disagree with your spouse. But you should disagree *respectfully*. Try to understand your spouse's perspective. Present the information that brought you to your opinion and listen to the information he or she brings. Entertain the possibility of changing your mind, instead of just trying to change your spouse's mind.

> *A disrespectful judgment occurs whenever someone tries to impose a system of values and beliefs on someone else.*

You see, each of us brings two things into a marriage: wisdom and foolishness. A marriage thrives when a husband and wife can blend their value systems, with each one's wisdom overriding the other's foolishness. By sharing their ideas and sorting through the pros and cons, a couple can create a belief system superior to what either partner had alone. But unless they approach the task with mutual respect—using respectful persuasion—the process won't work and they'll destroy their love for each other.

Respectful persuasion works like this: you begin by expressing respect for the perspective that your spouse already has and learning to understand why your spouse has it. Then you suggest an alternative perspective that you think will be in your spouse's best interest and not just in your own best interest. Finally, if your spouse is willing, you may need to do a test to prove your point. This may allow your spouse to see how useful the alternative belief can be. But in the final analysis, regardless of your evidence, the choice to change beliefs should be completely up to your spouse.

Imagine yourself as a refrigerator salesperson. How should you go about convincing a couple to buy your refrigerator? Would you go to their house, take one look at their refrigerator, and tell them that it's a piece of junk? Would that land you a sale? Not very likely. Instead, you and all your brochures would probably be thrown out of the house.

If you really wanted to make a sale, you would first try to understand your customers' needs. Then, without criticizing their refrigerator, you would explain the benefits of your refrigerator and how it would meet those needs. You would let the couple decide whether the benefits you present would make buying a new refrigerator worthwhile. Then, if they decided to keep their existing refrigerator, you would respect that decision so that someday, when they have a change of heart, the couple might buy their next one from you.

Respectful persuasion doesn't guarantee that you will win over your spouse to your perspective. It does guarantee, however, that you won't alienate him or her with your arrogant tactics. And the discussion may lead to a change of perspective on your part.

When a husband and wife present conflicting perspectives on an issue, I use the analogy of two people standing back to back viewing the horizon. They both see an entirely different scene—one is viewing the ocean and the other the mountains. Who's correct? In many conflicts I've witnessed between spouses, they've both had a valid point. By blending their perspectives with respect toward each other, they both come to understand the issue with far greater wisdom.

When Sue asked Jon to come home, she wasn't inviting him to lecture her or to try to straighten her out. She did not want Jon to remind her of the mistakes she had made. She wanted to give their marriage a fresh start and she wanted to be convinced that Jon would help her create a better marriage. So it was important for Jon to understand that he had to avoid anything that Sue would interpret as a disrespectful judgment. To help him out, Sue gladly offered to bring instances of his disrespect to his attention. Whenever she did, he apologized. Sue agreed to do the same when Jon felt she was being disrespectful of him.

Angry Outbursts: Deliberate attempts to hurt the other because of anger, usually in the form of verbal or physical attacks.

Jon was very angry with the way Sue had treated him, and Sue was angry, too. She felt that all of her problems were Jon's fault. She would not have fallen in love with Greg if Jon had not left her alone so much of the time.

When anger wins, love loses.

Sue and Jon needed to protect each other from their anger. If they didn't, their marital recovery would be impossible.

What makes you angry? Anger usually occurs when you don't get what you want. It begins with frustration and eventually leads you to the conclusion that your unhappiness is someone's fault. In your angry state, you are convinced that reasoning won't work and that the offender needs to be taught a lesson. Punishment is the answer, you assume.

An angry outburst offers you a simple way to punish the troublemaker. If your spouse is the troublemaker, your anger will urge you to hurt the one you've promised to protect. When you're angry, you don't care about your spouse's feelings. You're willing to scorch the culprit if it helps even the score.

But in the end, you have nothing to gain from an angry outburst. Punishment does not solve marital problems, it only makes your punished spouse want to inflict punishment on you—or leave you. Your spouse may rise to the challenge and try to destroy you in retaliation. But when anger wins, love loses.

Each of us has an arsenal of weapons we use when we're angry. If we think someone deserves to be punished, we unlock the gate and select an appropriate weapon. Sometimes the weapons are verbal (ridicule and sarcasm), sometimes they're devious plots to cause suffering, and sometimes they're physical. But they all have one thing in common: they're intended to hurt people. Since our spouse is at such close range, we can use our weapons to hurt him or her the most.

Some of the husbands and wives I've counseled have fairly harmless arsenals, maybe just a few awkward efforts at ridicule. Others are armed to nuclear proportions, actually putting their spouse's life in danger. The more dangerous your weapons are, the more important it is to control your temper. If you've ever lost your temper in a way that has caused your spouse great pain and suffering, you know that you cannot afford to lose your temper again. You must go to extreme lengths to protect your spouse from yourself.

Remember, in marriage you can be your spouse's greatest source of pleasure, but you can also be your spouse's greatest source of pain, particularly when he or she receives the brunt of your angry outburst.

It was easy for Jon and Sue to begin blaming each other for the nightmare they had experienced because they were both upset with each other. And it was difficult to keep their arsenals of weapons locked up. But by agreeing to avoid angry outbursts, they avoided one of the most dangerous threats to their marital recovery.

The three Love Busters I have just discussed, demands, disrespect, and anger, all have something in common—they represent controlling attempts to get our way and they are abusive. They should have no place in marriage because they harm spouses whenever they're used. But the next three Love Busters also have something in common—they have a devastating effect on marital compatibility.

Annoying Habits: Repeated behavior (mannerisms) that unintentionally causes the other to be unhappy.

When was the last time your spouse did something that annoyed you? Last week? Yesterday? An hour ago? Maybe your spouse is humming that irritating tune this very minute!

One of the most annoying things about an annoying habit is that it doesn't seem all that important—but it still drives you crazy! It's not abuse or abandonment, just annoyance. You should be able to shrug it off, but you can't. It's like the steady drip-drip-drip of water torture. Annoying habits can nickel and dime your Love Bank into bankruptcy.

When we're annoyed, we usually think others are being inconsiderate, particularly when we've explained to them that their behavior bothers us and yet they continue to do it. It's not just the behavior itself, but the thought behind it—the idea that they just don't care.

Annoying habits can nickel and dime your Love Bank into bankruptcy.

But when our behavior annoys others, we don't see the problem. It's just a little thing, we argue, so why can't other people adjust?

Throughout Jon and Sue's marriage, Jon was with Sue so seldom that his annoying habits had little impact on his account in Sue's Love Bank. But now that they were trying to reconcile, and I had instructed them to spend a considerable amount of time together, Jon's annoying habits became immediately apparent to Sue. Instead of appreciating the effort he was making to meet her emotional needs, all she could think about was his constant sniffing.

Annoying habits can drive a wedge between you and your spouse. But since these habits are unintentional, it's often assumed that nothing can or should be done about them. And yet, they give the distinct impression to the one who's annoyed that you're incompatible. Who wants to be with someone whose habits are annoying?

But how should you go about changing your habits so that they are no longer annoying?

It begins with the realization that whenever you do something that bothers your spouse, you are withdrawing love units. Tell each other that eliminating annoying behaviors is a high priority for both of you, identify them if they exist, and then get to work eliminating them.

The Love Busters Questionnaire that I had Sue and Jon complete asked them to provide a list of each other's habits that they found annoying. Jon left his list blank because he was not annoyed enough by anything that Sue did to mention it. Sue, on the other hand, had a long list for Jon to try to eliminate.

This discrepancy, women finding men more annoying than men, is common in most marriages. So men will often think that it's a woman's problem—*she's too easily annoyed*. Instead of solving it, he feels that she should learn to be less annoyed.

But I take the opposite position. It's the problem of the person who is annoying. Unless Jon addressed Sue's complaints about his annoying habits, he would continue making Love Bank withdrawals whenever they were together. The only way to avoid that outcome was to learn to stop doing whatever it was that annoyed her.

Since the list of his annoying habits was fairly long, I suggested that Sue prioritize them. Which habits were the most annoying? Which habits should Jon try to overcome first? I gave Jon the assignment of focusing his attention on the three most annoying habits at a time. When they were overcome, he would then tackle the next three on her list.

Knowing that Jon was taking her complaints seriously was very encouraging to Sue, to say nothing about the fact that he was able to start eliminating the habits that annoyed her most immediately.

Dishonesty: Failure to reveal to the other correct information, or leaving a false impression, about emotional reactions, personal history, daily activities, and plans for the future.

As Sue's affair was developing, she became increasingly dishonest with Jon. Instead of telling him how she was feeling about Greg, she lied about their relationship. Then, when Jon first learned that Sue had been unfaithful, and when he first confronted her with the evidence, she lied about the affair. Jon still remembered the look in her eye when she lied to him. He wasn't sure what upset him the most, her affair or her dishonesty about it.

Without a doubt, dishonesty in any form, even "little white lies," makes massive Love Bank withdrawals.

For Sue, her dishonesty about her affair was about as addictive as the affair itself. One lie led to another until even she became confused as to what was really true. By the time they counseled with me, Jon didn't think he could ever again believe anything Sue said. And without trust, how could he ever have a fulfilling marriage?

But dishonesty does more than make massive Love Bank withdrawals. It also strangles compatibility. It offers misleading information that makes it

Dishonesty in any form makes massive Love Bank withdrawals.

impossible to understand each other. To create and sustain compatibility, you must lay your cards on the table. You must be honest about your thoughts, feelings, habits, likes, dislikes, personal history, daily activities, and plans for the future. When misinformation is part of the mix, you have little hope of making successful adjustments to each other.

Dishonesty makes solutions to problems hard to find, and it often leaves couples ignorant of the problems themselves. Sue's reluctance to tell Jon how unfulfilled she had become because of his neglect made her vulnerable to Greg, who was all too willing to fill the void. If Jon had heard a play-by-play accounting of how she felt about their marriage, and how she was becoming attracted to Greg, he would have done something about the problem before it overtook them. But he was left ignorant by Sue's dishonesty.

There's another very important reason to be honest. Honesty tends to make our behavior more thoughtful. If we knew that everything we do and say would be recorded and watched by all our friends, we would be far less likely to engage in thoughtless acts. Criminals would not steal and commit violent acts as often if they knew their actions were recorded. Honesty is the video recording in our lives. We know what we do, and if we are honest about what we do, we tend not to engage in thoughtless acts because we know those acts will be revealed—by ourselves.

In an honest relationship, thoughtless acts are usually corrected. Bad habits are nipped in the bud. Honesty keeps a couple from drifting into incompatibility—as incompatible attitudes and behaviors are revealed, they can become targets for elimination. But if these attitudes and behaviors remain hidden, they are left to grow out of control.

Independent Behavior: Activities of a spouse that are conceived and executed as if the other spouse did not exist.

Dishonesty played a very important role in the development of Sue's affair. But independent behavior played an equally important role. The decisions she made that led to her affair, and helped it develop, were thoughtless.

If you make decisions without considering the effect they'll have on your spouse, your activities will make you impossible to live with. And if you are dishonest about what you do because you don't want to give those things up, you develop a secret way of life that ultimately grows into a monster. Sooner or later, when this secret second life is discovered, you deal your spouse the double Love Buster of engaging in thoughtless behavior *and* being dishonest about it.

The lifestyle you create with the decisions you make will make or break your marriage. If you make decisions that take each other's feelings into account, you will create a lifestyle that makes you both happy—you will have created a compatible lifestyle. But if you make thoughtless decisions behind your spouse's back, hoping that your spouse will not discover the secret lifestyle you are creating, you will create an incompatible lifestyle, one that you and your spouse cannot enjoy together.

These last two Love Busters, dishonesty and independent behavior, will prevent you and your spouse from enjoying your life together. We are all tempted to make decisions that are in our own best interest, ignoring the best interest of our spouse. And we are also tempted to keep secret details of ourselves that reflect our weaknesses or might get us into trouble. But if you want to stay in love with each other, you cannot afford to tolerate them in your marriage. In the end, these Love Busters will drain all the love units from your Love Banks and leave you miserable.

Completing the Love Busters Questionnaire

Now that you understand what the six Love Busters are, and how they can each ruin marriages, I want you to complete a form I mentioned in the last chapter, the Love Busters Questionnaire. It's one of the three forms that Jon and Sue completed to help them create a plan for recovery that was tailor-made for them. I designed this form to help couples identify their habits that make substantial Love Bank withdrawals.

This form analyzes each Love Buster with a series of questions. The first question asks how much unhappiness it causes you in your marriage. If it is not a problem, it's not a Love Buster for you to address, and so you can skip the remaining questions. But if it causes you unhappiness, your spouse should know how often it happens (question B), the form(s) that it takes (question C), the worst form (question D), when it started (question E), and how it has developed over time (question F).

At the end of the questionnaire, you are asked to rate the Love Busters according to the unhappiness they create. While all Love Busters should be eliminated, it makes sense to eliminate the most painful Love Busters first.

The results of these questionnaires will help you understand the pain and unhappiness you cause each other. When you are a source of your spouse's unhappiness, you not only make Love Bank withdrawals, but you encourage your spouse to build emotional defenses that make him or her withdraw from you emotionally. These emotional defenses prevent you from making Love Bank deposits to make up for the loss. It's only when you overcome Love Busters that the emotional barrier is removed and you're in a position to meet your spouse's emotional needs. That's why our program of recovery usually begins with the elimination of Love Busters.

After you read this chapter, I encourage you to make two copies of the questionnaire, one for each of you. (They can be enlarged and copied either from appendix C or from the Questionnaires section of MarriageBuilders. com.) When you have completed the forms, give them to each other to read.

When you read your spouse's reactions to these habits, remember that they provide information regarding Love Bank withdrawals that are ruining your love for each other. Don't justify them or defend yourself for having them. Instead, get right to work eliminating them.

A Closer Look at Dishonesty and Independent Behavior

Since so many couples I counsel are confused about how honest spouses should be with each other, I have created a policy to explain it. I call it the Policy of Radical Honesty, because so many think it's radical. But from my perspective either you are honest or you are dishonest. There is no middle ground. So in the next chapter, I will explain this policy to you, and try to justify something so radical that there are many who feel it should not be followed. And yet, without honesty—radical honesty—your recovery will have little hope for success, and you are very unlikely to be in love with each other throughout your lives together.

Another Love Buster that deserves special attention is independent behavior. All six Love Busters should be eliminated in marriage, but as is the case with dishonesty, independent behavior also plays a special role in making affairs possible. So in chapter 10, I'll explain how to have a compatible marriage that's completely free of independent behavior.

9

Avoid Withdrawals, Part II

Overcome Dishonesty

*T*he two Love Busters that made Sue's affair last as long as it did were dishonesty and independent behavior. Together they helped create a secret second life that prolonged the agony for everyone involved.

But Kevin took a different path. When he knew he was in love with Amy, he thought about lying to Lee about it, but it didn't take him long to reject that option. By honestly expressing his feelings about Amy to his wife, he avoided the year of agony that Sue and Jon had to bear. If Sue had taken the path of honesty when she first became aware of her feelings toward Greg, she too could have avoided most of the misery that she imposed on herself and her family.

Honesty is essential for marital recovery after an affair. It not only points a couple toward their goal of reconciliation, but it also helps restore trust. Of course, honesty is essential to creating a great marriage—period. But almost all affairs *require* dishonesty. An honest relationship between a husband and wife plus an avoidance of independent behavior, which I'll be discussing in the next chapter, makes affairs almost impossible. So if a couple has any hope of recovering trust after an affair, they must create a level of honesty never before achieved in their marriage.

To help spouses understand how honest they should be with each other, I've created the Policy of Radical Honesty.

The Policy of Radical Honesty

Reveal to your spouse as much information about yourself as you know—your thoughts, feelings, habits, likes, dislikes, past history, daily activities, and future plans.

You may agree with me that spouses should be honest with each other, but you may wonder how far honesty should go. My advice is for it to go all the way. That's why I call it *radical* honesty. I encourage spouses to become transparent to each other. So to help couples understand what radical honesty really is, I have broken it down into five parts:

1. *Emotional honesty.* Reveal your emotional reactions—both positive and negative—to the events of your life, particularly to your spouse's behavior.
2. *Historical honesty.* Reveal information about your personal history, particularly events that demonstrate personal weakness or failure.
3. *Current honesty.* Reveal information about the events of your day. Provide your spouse with a calendar of your activities, with special emphasis on those that may affect your spouse.
4. *Future honesty.* Reveal your thoughts and plans regarding future activities and objectives.

To some extent this rule seems like motherhood and apple pie. Who would argue that it's *not* a good idea? But in my years of experience as a marriage counselor, I have found that many clients consider dishonesty a good idea under certain circumstances.

Granted, dishonesty may seem like a good short-term solution to marital conflict. It'll probably get you off the hook for a few days or months. But it's a terrible long-term solution. If you expect to build a relationship of trust that will last throughout your life, total honesty is essential.

To those who argue that dishonesty can be justified under certain circumstances, I disagree. There should be no room for exceptions. But because there are so many who advocate partial dishonesty in marriage, I need to build a case for my position. Let's take a careful look at each of the five parts of this rule, beginning with emotional honesty.

Emotional Honesty

Sue found it very difficult to express her emotional reactions, particularly the negative ones. She was afraid that Jon would judge her and she certainly did not want Jon to be hurt by those feelings. She did not feel capable of expressing negative feelings without anger, disrespect, or demands. So she didn't express them at all.

Sue also felt that any revelation of negative reactions would reflect the fact that she did not accept Jon unconditionally. She wanted unconditional acceptance from him and she thought that her own negative reactions would encourage him to be critical of her.

But negative feelings, like frustration, loneliness, and discontentment, serve a valuable purpose in marriage. They are a signal that something is wrong. If Sue had learned to steer clear of angry outbursts, disrespectful judgments, and selfish demands, her honest expression of negative reactions would have alerted Jon to an adjustment that would have made their marriage much more enjoyable.

Emotional Honesty

Reveal your emotional reactions—both positive and negative—to the events of your life, particularly to your spouse's behavior.

Emotional honesty provides an alternative to either sweeping a problem under the rug or using demands, disrespect, or anger to get the problem on the table. It is the simple expression of a negative reaction in the form of a complaint: *It makes me feel bad.*

A complaint is a statement of how you feel when your spouse does something that bothers you: *It bothers me when you put your feet up on the coffee table.* But it turns into a selfish demand when you tell your spouse what to do about it: *Take your feet off the coffee table right now!* If you were to add a disrespectful judgment to the complaint, it would become a criticism: *Didn't your mother ever teach you to keep your feet off the furniture?* Escalating the demand and judgment one more notch into an angry outburst might find you yelling obscenities at your spouse.

To improve a complaint's effectiveness, I recommend adding a statement that reveals what you desire in terms of a specific, positive behavior. I call it an "I'd love it if" statement. For example, *I'd love it if you would keep your feet on the floor or find a footstool for your feet.* Many of my clients use this emotional honesty format because it shares what a person would like, rather than only sharing what is not liked.

But the mere communication of a complaint or suggestion of a positive alternative behavior does not assure that all the necessary adjustments will be made. There is still work to do, and in the next chapter I'll teach you how to solve problems that are raised when you communicate your grievances. But without that honest communication, failure is guaranteed.

To adjust successfully and avoid maladjustment, you need a steady flow of accurate data from each other. Without this, unhappy situations can go on and on. When choices are based on faulty information, mistakes abound. But if you communicate your feelings to each other accurately, you can correct your mistakes before they withdraw too many love units.

Honesty enables couples to make appropriate adjustments to each other, and adjustment is what a good marriage is all about. Jon and Sue needed to adjust to each other as their surroundings and their needs changed. But how could they adjust without accurate information from each other? That's flying blind—like a pilot whose instrument panel has shorted out.

The expression of negative reactions is important, but don't overlook the expression of positive reactions. Using the "feet on the coffee table" example, it would be helpful to acknowledge appreciation when the footstool is used. And whenever you enjoy something that your spouse does for you, be sure to express that feeling to him or her. While positive feelings are generally easier to communicate than negative ones, many couples miss that opportunity.

Historical Honesty

Your personal history holds significant information about you—information about your strengths and weaknesses. Your spouse needs to fully understand both your good and bad characteristics. Under what conditions are you the most caring and considerate? Where are you likely to be most self-centered and hurtful?

History tends to repeat itself. For example, if a man has had problems controlling his temper in the past, it's likely he'll have the same struggle in the future. If a woman has been chemically dependent in the past, she'll be susceptible to drug or alcohol abuse in the future. If you talk openly about your past mistakes, your spouse will understand your weaknesses and together you can avoid situations that will tend to create problems for you in the future.

Historical Honesty

Reveal information about your personal history, particularly events that demonstrate personal weakness or failure.

No area of your life should be kept secret. All questions asked by your spouse should be answered fully and completely. Periods of poor adjustment in your past should be given special attention. Be sure that both you and your spouse understand what happened in those previous circumstances. That way you will be able to create a lifestyle together that does not tempt your weaknesses.

Not only should *you* explain your past to your spouse, but you should encourage your spouse to gather information from those who knew you before. I have encouraged couples who are considering marriage to meet with several significant people from each other's past. It's often quite an eye-opener!

But if I tell her about all the bad things I've done, she'll never trust me again.

If he finds out about my past, he'll be crushed. It will ruin his whole image of me.

I have heard these protests from various clients—ashamed of things they had done. *Why dig it all up? Let old mistakes stay buried in ancient history! Why not just leave that little demon alone?* I answer that it's not a "little demon," but an extremely important part of their personal story and it says something about their character.

Maybe you don't really want to be known for who you are. That's the saddest position of all. It means you would rather keep your secret than experience one of life's greatest joys—to be loved and accepted in spite of known weaknesses or past mistakes.

As Sue and Jon learned to be fully transparent with each other, they began to reveal some of the significant events of their past that they had kept secret. When they first came to me for counseling, I had them complete my Personal History Questionnaire, which systematically reviewed many of the significant events of their past. I asked them to share their questionnaires with each other and feel free to ask any questions that would be triggered by them.

The Personal History Questionnaire is available to you free of charge in the Questionnaires section of MarriageBuilders.com. Make two copies of it, one for each of you, and answer them as honestly as you can. Leave nothing out and be willing to pursue any line of inquiry with your spouse that will help you understand each other better.

One of the most important historical events in Sue's life was her affair. So I asked Jon to write the questions about her affair that he felt were still unanswered. They scheduled a time for her to answer those questions honestly and openly. I encouraged Jon to avoid "why" questions because they had already been answered (Jon had failed to meet her emotional needs, leaving her vulnerable. Sue had made an incredibly selfish, dishonest, and cruel decision because she thought it was in her best interest at the time).

I told Jon to avoid bringing up further questions after Sue had answered the ones he gave her. One of the biggest mistakes made by couples trying to reconcile is to keep talking about the affair. By dwelling on it, the negative memories of the past are brought into the present for no useful purpose.

Current Honesty

After eight years of marriage, Sue found herself in love with another man. She did not develop her friendship with Greg because she wanted to have an affair. Quite the contrary—she didn't want an affair at all. But once she was in love with Greg, an affair seemed inevitable. She did nothing to stop it, and her dishonesty made it all possible.

Sue spent an increasing amount of time with Greg because she loved him. But to keep Jon in the dark, she had to lie about the time they spent together. It was only after he found them making love that Jon realized she had been living a secret second life. Dishonesty had become a habit for her.

Kevin, on the other hand, had been in the habit of revealing his daily schedule to Lee. If he had decided to pursue his affair with Amy, he would have had to *learn* to be dishonest about how he spent his time. That's one of the reasons he told Lee about his affair as soon as it started and why it was possible for him to end it quickly—because he was not in the habit of being dishonest. Current honesty made it easier for Kevin to end his affair than for Sue to end hers.

I explained to Sue and Jon that current honesty requires complete transparency. Nothing should be hidden. Passwords, email, text messages, phone logs, computer histories, and all other forms of communication should be made available to a spouse. It's not punishment for Sue's affair—a lifetime prison sentence. It's the formula for a very fulfilling marriage. It provides a level of understanding that's necessary for a couple to make wise decisions.

Current Honesty

Reveal information about the events of your day. Provide your spouse with a calendar of your activities, with special emphasis on those that may affect your spouse.

Besides giving Jon access to her various forms of communication, Sue also gave him a twenty-four-hours-a-day schedule of her whereabouts, and Jon did the same. In good marriages couples become so interdependent that sharing a daily schedule is essential to their coordination of activities. In weak marriages, however, couples are reluctant to reveal their schedules, because they are often engaged in activities that would offend each other. Assuming that their spouse would object to these activities, they hide the details of their day, telling themselves, *What he doesn't know won't hurt him*, or *She's happier not knowing everything*.

Even when activities are innocent, it's extremely important for your spouse to understand what you do with your time, because almost everything you do will affect your spouse in some way. Make sure you are easy to find in an emergency or when your spouse just wants to say hello during the day.

At first, Sue felt very uncomfortable giving Jon her twenty-four-hours-a-day schedule and revealing all of her communication passwords and information. She had felt comfortable keeping it all secret, even when there was nothing to hide. Now she felt vulnerable and exposed.

Admittedly, it takes awhile to adjust to transparency, and during the adjustment Sue was very annoyed. She understood why it was necessary. It gave Jon some reassurance that she wasn't rekindling her affair, and it also helped him understand her. But she didn't like having to account for her time and activities.

Besides, she was now required to consider Jon's feelings whenever she did anything. Before her affair, she had made most of her decisions without having to discuss them with Jon first. Now she felt that she was married to her parole officer. But as these new habits of current honesty became familiar to her, her past independent lifestyle became foreign to her. It wasn't long before her feeling of being trapped disappeared.

Future Honesty

Kevin's honesty about his future plans was crucial to his success in ending his affair. He was in love with Amy and they planned to deepen their relationship. By revealing those plans to Lee, he took the first step toward saving his marriage. Because he considered Lee's feelings before he implemented any of his plans with Amy, those future plans were eliminated.

Sue, on the other hand, had not been in the habit of revealing her plans to Jon before her affair. That's part of the reason her affair was so difficult to end. But even as they were trying to restore their marriage after the affair, she had trouble being honest about her plans. She was in the habit of making her plans independently of Jon, and bringing him into those plans felt very uncomfortable. By including him in her planning process, she thought he would have too much influence over her. She wanted to think her plans through on her own, and then, maybe, she would share her final decisions with him.

Future Honesty

Reveal your thoughts and plans regarding future
activities and objectives.

After I've made such a big issue of revealing past indiscretions, you can imagine how I feel about revealing future plans that may get you into trouble. Future plans are much easier to discuss than past mistakes or failures, yet, like Sue, many spouses keep their plans secret from each other. Why? Some people believe that communicating future plans just gives a spouse the opportunity to stop them. They have their sights set on a certain goal and they don't want anything to stand in their way.

When you fail to tell your spouse about your plans, you're not being honest. You may be trying to avoid trouble in the present, but eventually the future will arrive, revealing your thoughtless plans. At that point your spouse will be hurt that you didn't take his or her feelings into account when you were making those plans.

If I wait for my wife to agree to my plans, a husband might say, *we'll never accomplish anything. She's so conservative; she never wants to take any risks, and so we miss every opportunity that comes along.* But if her feelings are important to him, he needs her input on his plans. Without it, he risks building a future where her interests are left behind.

Oh, but the plans I make are best for both of us, a wife might say. *He may not understand my decision now but once he sees how things turn out, he'll thank me for going ahead with it.* Her plan of action is disrespectful. It assumes the husband's judgment is so poor that his wife must make his decisions for him. She would not want him to be that disrespectful of her judgments, and yet her example may very well lead to that outcome.

Whatever your reason for keeping your spouse in the dark about your plans, your decision will eventually give you more trouble than it's worth. And when it's discovered, Love Bank withdrawals are the result.

Information about gifts or plans for special occasions may be the rare exception to future honesty. But in the recovery of your relationship after an affair, I would not be dishonest even under these special conditions until your marriage is completely restored. When you plan to give each other gifts, you should explain your plans and then ask, *How do you feel about what I am planning to give you?* Honesty in your marriage is so important right now that you cannot afford to keep secrets from each other even when they may seem harmless.

How Well Does Your Spouse Really Know You?

Do you feel that you're misunderstood? Your problem may be due to your failure to be completely honest with your spouse. If your spouse seems to have a false impression about your thoughts, feelings, habits, likes, dislikes, personal history, daily activities, or plans for the future, do you try to clear it up? Or do you leave your spouse with a false impression? Do you provide information about yourself that your spouse wouldn't think to ask?

I ask probing questions when I counsel. And I probe most deeply in areas where people tend to leave false impressions. Since most marital problems originate with serious misconceptions, I do what I can to dig out these little weeds that eventually choke the plant. It goes without saying that false impressions are just as deceitful as outright lies.

The purpose of radical honesty is to have the facts in front of you. Without them, you'll fail to solve the simplest marital problems. Lying to your spouse or even giving false impressions will leave your spouse ignorant of the facts.

In Sue and Jon's marriage, one of the biggest false impressions was that they were doing an outstanding job meeting each other's needs. This form of deceit is often tempting, especially early in marriage. They were both dissatisfied, but didn't want to appear unappreciative. They felt that showing admiration, even though it was false, would help their marriage.

As I mentioned earlier, you can minimize the loss of love units by expressing your dissatisfaction in nonthreatening, nonjudgmental ways. You can show appreciation for the effort made to meet your needs and then provide an alternative behavior that offers guidance for making that effort more effective. But only a true expression of your feelings will help you find a solution to your problems. Whenever you do not reveal the complete truth, you cripple your spouse's ability to meet your needs. You provide a map that leads to failure. Truth is the only map that can lead to success.

Creating an Environment for Radical Honesty

Sue needed to learn to be honest with Jon. But Jon needed to learn how to create an environment where her honesty would be encouraged. I wanted him to reward her for her honesty. In the past he had done the opposite. In the very few times that she complained about feeling lonely and unfulfilled, he responded by suggesting that she should appreciate what she had instead of complaining about what she didn't have.

Don't criticize your spouse when you hear the truth about how he or she feels. That simply encourages dishonesty the next time. Instead, talk about how important honesty is to you and how you want to work together to achieve greater love and compatibility. Use the disclosure as evidence that you both need to rise to a new level of fulfillment.

How well do you encourage honesty? You may say that you want your spouse to be honest, but do your own values promote it? How do you answer the following questions?

1. If the truth is terribly upsetting to you, do you want your spouse to be honest only at a time when you are emotionally prepared?
2. Do you keep some aspects of your life secret and do you encourage your spouse to respect your privacy or boundaries in those areas?
3. Do you have well-defined informational boundaries that you encourage your spouse not to cross?
4. Do you like to create a certain mystery between you and your spouse?
5 Are there subjects or situations where you would want to avoid radical honesty?

If you answer *yes* to any of these questions, you do not always value honesty. In certain situations, you feel your marriage is better off with dishonesty. You see, there are always "reasons" to be dishonest. But that little crack is all dishonesty needs to slip into your marriage and cause erosion. As soon as you allow one reason for dishonesty, it becomes easier to allow others, and before you know it, you have a dishonest relationship.

You encourage honesty when you *value* honesty. If your own values do not consistently support honesty, you will be sending each other mixed messages that will undermine the Policy of Radical Honesty.

Having consistent values is one way to encourage honesty. But another important way to encourage it is in the way you react to honesty. Do your reactions convey an appreciation for the truth, even if it's painful? These questions will help you determine if you are actually discouraging honesty in the way you sometimes react to it.

1. Do you ever make selfish demands when your spouse is honest with you?
2. Do you ever make disrespectful judgments when your spouse is honest with you?
3. Do you ever have angry outbursts when your spouse is honest with you?

If you answered *yes* to any of these questions, you are using Love Busters to punish honesty and you are inadvertently encouraging dishonesty. The way to encourage each other to be truthful is to minimize the negative consequences of truthful revelations. Instead of trying to punish your spouse when a shocking truth is revealed, try to reward your spouse's honesty.

I have taught couples to say, *Thank you for being honest with me.* If they feel they need some time to process the new information, so as to protect their spouse from any Love Buster, I have them add, *Can I have ten minutes to think about this and then we'll get back together to talk about it?*

You encourage honesty when you value honesty.

There are some marriages so infected by the Love Buster of angry outbursts that it is not safe to be honest. Honesty runs the risk of a severe beating or even death. In these marriages, I suggest that a couple separate until safety can be assured. No couple should live together as long as one spouse persists in abusing the other. And if honesty triggers physical or emotional abuse, separation is usually the only reasonable response.

Remember, honesty is never your enemy; it's a friend that brings light to a problem that often needs a creative solution. If honesty is followed by safe and pleasant negotiation, it becomes the necessary first step toward improving your compatibility and love for each other.

Don't Wrap Your Honesty in Love Busters

Not only can a spouse's reaction to honesty be a Love Buster, but the honest revelation itself can also be a Love Buster.

Imagine if you were to express your unhappiness by saying, *If you don't start spending more time with me soon, I'll find someone else to spend time with and you'll be sleeping with your money.* You're being honest in communicating your unhappiness with being left alone, but you're wrapping it in a selfish demand. It's an ultimatum with a threat of punishment if the demand is not met.

Alternately, instead of making a demand, you might say, *I'm the least important person in your life. Your priorities are certainly screwed up. You seem to think that money is more important than I am.* That may be your honest opinion, but you're expressing it in a disrespectful way. Instead of getting the help you need from your spouse, you're more likely to start an argument about priorities.

Or you might throw a lamp and cry out, *You never have time for me anymore. I don't know why I ever married you, you selfish jerk.* Your honesty would get lost in your angry outburst. It does little good to express genuine feelings if your spouse is running for cover.

There are better ways to express your honest feelings. You should say, *I become upset when I'm left alone at night. I'd love it if we could spend more time together. Can we talk about ways to make this happen?* These are honest statements of your feelings, because you are telling your spouse how you feel and what you would like, and you are suggesting the creation of a plan to see that it happens.

Sometimes it feels awkward to avoid selfish demands, disrespectful judgments, and angry outbursts. You may have used them to express your dissatisfaction so often that they may seem to be a part of your normal conversation. But with practice, anyone can learn to express their honest feelings and reactions without using them. And once they are no longer a part of your conversation, the chances that your spouse will listen to you and work with you to resolve your conflicts are greatly increased.

10

Avoid Withdrawals, Part III

Overcome Independent
Behavior

*I*n the last chapter, I identified dishonesty as one of two Love Busters that makes affairs—and a secret second life—possible. In this chapter, I'll identify the other: independent behavior. Independent behavior is planning and executing activities as if your spouse doesn't exist. It's doing what you please regardless of how it will affect your spouse.

Can a marriage thrive if spouses ignore each other's reactions to what they do? Anyone who's been married, even for only a day, can testify that ignoring each other's reactions leads to some very unpleasant interactions. That's why I call independent behavior a Love Buster: it causes Love Bank withdrawals for the spouse whose feelings have not been considered. And when those withdrawals are made, the offended spouse usually responds with anger, causing even more withdrawals.

To avoid the angry reaction, a thoughtless spouse often reverts to behaving independently in secret. They don't tell their spouse what they're doing, which adds the Love Buster dishonesty to their offensive behavior. Infidelity is one of the most painful examples of how this happens. They think that as long as their spouse is ignorant of their thoughtlessness, it won't create a negative reaction.

But a secret second life has a way of eventually becoming exposed. And when it is, withdrawals cascade from a betrayed spouse's Love Bank.

To prevent the suffering that independent behavior causes, I recommend *inter*dependent behavior: *Activities of a spouse that are conceived and executed with the interests of both spouses in mind.* When spouses make their decisions interdependently, the risk of an affair—and a host of other destructive behavior—is eliminated.

Interdependent Behavior

Activities of a spouse that are conceived and executed with
the interests of both spouses in mind.

Many of Jon's and Sue's decisions that had caused each other's unhappiness were innocent. They had not realized they were thoughtless. For example, Jon's time spent away from his family developing a career was thoughtless because it had made Sue feel very unhappy. But Jon did it in an effort to provide his family with a higher standard of living. Jon thought Sue appreciated his hard work, but she actually resented it and it became a major cause of withdrawals from his account in her Love Bank.

I gave Jon and Sue a rule to follow that would change their independent behavior into interdependent behavior. I call it the Policy of Joint Agreement.

The Policy of Joint Agreement

Never do anything without an enthusiastic agreement
between you and your spouse.

This policy unmasks thoughtless behavior. Anything done without this mutual agreement is likely to cause unhappiness for one of the spouses. If Jon and Sue were willing to avoid being the cause of each other's unhappiness, they had to talk about the things they planned to do before they did them and hear each other's honest reactions to those plans. The plan could not move forward until an enthusiastic agreement was reached.

The Policy of Joint Agreement, combined with the Policy of Radical Honesty, not only helped them eliminate the possibility of behavior they knew to be thoughtless, like infidelity, but also eliminated behavior that may have seemed innocent to the one who did it but turned out to be hurtful.

Thoughtfulness: The Goal of Marital Negotiation

Jon and Sue both agreed with me that they needed to stop making decisions that were good for one and bad for the other. They agreed that the gains from having a mutually agreeable lifestyle more than outweighed the personal loss of making independent decisions. They learned to ask each other *How would you feel?* before they made any decision.

That's the first step toward marital negotiation—asking the question "How would you feel?" Without it, couples don't negotiate. They simply make their decisions without regard for each other's feelings. But by following the Policy of Joint Agreement, Sue and Jon guaranteed each other that they would negotiate, because they couldn't do anything until they were both in agreement. The Policy of Joint Agreement changed the way they discussed issues, and for the first time in their marriage they were communicating with the deepest concern for each other's feelings.

In most marriages, negotiation is tough. Whenever there is a conflict of opinions, spouses usually either do whatever they're asked or refuse to do much of anything. Discussing each conflict until a mutually enthusiastic agreement is reached is very unusual. But that's because most spouses are unskilled in negotiating with each other. They don't know how to work out agreements that are in their mutual interest.

However, if a couple is committed to avoid any decision until they come to a mutually enthusiastic agreement, eventually they learn how to negotiate, and then they do it almost effortlessly. They become very creative in discovering solutions to problems, and this leads to their mutual happiness.

The Policy of Joint Agreement forced Jon and Sue to negotiate until they could arrive at a decision that would not hurt either of them. It forced them to be thoughtful. These mutually acceptable decisions formed the foundation for a new lifestyle that they would share with each other—a lifestyle that would not withdraw love units from either of their Love Banks.

How to Negotiate with the Policy of Joint Agreement

Throughout Jon and Sue's marriage the issue of his business travel had been a source of unhappiness for Sue. She was lonely when he was away from home. Now Jon had a new position that didn't require traveling, but it paid quite a bit less and they both missed his higher income. Sue wanted Jon's previous income without the problems his travel caused. Jon and Sue needed to find a solution to this dilemma, so it was on this issue that I taught them to negotiate with the Policy of Joint Agreement.

There are four guidelines that I recommend to couples for reaching an enthusiastic agreement. I encouraged Jon and Sue to use them as they discussed his career alternatives.

Guideline 1: Set Ground Rules to Make Negotiations Pleasant and Safe

Before you start to negotiate, agree with each other that you will both follow these rules: (a) be pleasant and cheerful throughout your discussion of the issue; (b) put safety first—do not make demands, show disrespect, or become angry when you negotiate, even if your negotiations fail; and (c) if you reach an impasse, stop for a while and come back to the issue later. A test I sometimes recommend to see if a couple is ready to make this time pleasant is for them to try to smile. If they can't smile, they should find another time to negotiate.

One spouse's criticism or pessimistic attitude will often trigger an escalation of negativity and pessimism from the other spouse. This can lead to Love Busters intruding on your conversation. Demands, disrespect, and anger will ruin any effort you make to negotiate. You will simply never have an enthusiastic agreement about anything if you hurt each other as you try to solve your problems. Instead, try to soothe each other when something said creates a negative reaction.

If your negotiation becomes unpleasant or unsafe to either of you, break it off and choose another time to discuss the issue. Do the same thing if it appears you have reached an impasse. Taking a break will allow tempers to cool, and may reveal new insights that can be discussed when you begin your negotiations again.

Guideline 2: Identify the Problem from the Perspectives of Both You and Your Spouse

Be able to state each other's position on the issue before you go on to find a solution. Each of you should describe what you would like and why you would like it, or why you might not want to fulfill your spouse's request. Then you should repeat each other's perspectives to be sure you understood them. I recommend keeping your perspectives as brief as possible so that you can accurately restate what each of you said in your own words. Don't simply mimic each other. Try to reflect an accurate comprehension of each other's perspectives. And keep trying to get it right until you both feel understood by each other. Respectful understanding of each other's perspectives is essential to reaching a mutually enthusiastic agreement.

As soon as Sue began to explain how she felt about Jon's trips away from home, she could hardly hold back her tears. She explained how she had wanted Jon to reach his highest potential with his job and earn a living that would create a comfortable lifestyle for their family. Yet whenever he was gone, she felt very lonely, as if he had abandoned her. She explained that while her needs were not being met when he traveled, her need for financial support was not being met by his new position that did not require travel. She wanted to find a solution that would enable him to meet all of her emotional needs.

After Sue explained her perspective, Jon summarized what he heard. When he was finished, Sue made a few minor corrections to clarify her perspective. But in general she was very pleased with Jon's summary and felt that he understood her position.

Then Jon described his perspective. He began by explaining how they had been living above their means for some time. Before the affair they had spent just about everything he earned. But during their separation their expenses skyrocketed. Jon had to borrow heavily to pay his own living expenses and pay the support to Sue that the court had ordered. It had left them on the verge of bankruptcy.

To add to this financial crisis, Jon had given up his high-paying position to take a lower-paying position that did not require travel. He did this while Sue was having her affair as an expression of his willingness and ability to meet her emotional needs when she would return to him.

After hearing Jon's perspective, Sue summarized what she heard. Jon was satisfied that it accurately reflected his feelings.

This was not the first time they had this conversation. But they had not understood each other's perspectives quite as clearly. And they had never gone beyond that second step of understanding each other's perspective. They knew what the problem was but they had never solved it. That's because the solutions that they had presented to each other only took their own interests into account. They had not tried to solve the problem in a way that would satisfy both of them. Now their financial crisis pushed them onto a fast track toward a solution to the problem. They had to come quickly to a mutually enthusiastic agreement.

Guideline 3: Brainstorm Solutions with Abandon

Give your brains the opportunity to do what they do best—solve problems. Think of all sorts of possible solutions that might be acceptable to both of you and write them all down. If you use your imaginations, you will have a long list of ideas to consider.

Jon and Sue wrote down these possible solutions:

1. Jon tries to find a higher paying job that does not require travel.
2. Jon stays in his current position that does not require travel. They adjust to his lower salary by lowering their standard of living, selling their home, and buying a more affordable home.
3. Jon stays in his current position and Sue works full-time to help pay off the debt and compensate for Jon's lower income.
4. Jon returns to his old position, but Sue travels with him—leaving the children with friends or family.
5. Jon returns to his old position until their debt is eliminated, but they live under a strict budget that would have their bills paid in two years. Whenever he travels, each day he calls Sue at least three times, engages in at least one and a half hours of conversation, and faxes her a letter. He gives her flowers before he leaves, brings her a gift when he returns, and goes away alone with Sue for a weekend after each trip. He limits his trips to only three nights away from home.

The longer they thought about the issues, the more creative they became. I encouraged them both to let their minds run wild and write down anything that occurred to them. Jon even suggested that he quit his job and that they all join the Peace Corps. Sue didn't criticize his idea. Instead, she just smiled.

Guideline 4: Choose a Solution That Is Appealing to Both of You

From your list of possible solutions, many will satisfy only one of you. However, scattered within the list will be solutions that both of you may find attractive. Among those solutions that are mutually satisfactory, select the one that you both like the most as the final solution to your problem. But if you can't find one that you can both agree to enthusiastically, go back to guideline 3 and brainstorm longer.

Before choosing a final solution, Jon and Sue took several days gathering information. Jon discovered that his old position, with its increased salary, was available to him if he wanted it back. Sue confirmed that her responsibilities at work were flexible and that she could join Jon on business trips once in a while. He also made a few telephone calls to see if he could work for another company in a position that did not require as much travel.

In the end, they enthusiastically agreed to a solution that combined several of their ideas. Their ultimate goal was for Jon to have a job that would decrease their debt yet give the family a high quality of life. That quality of life was to include Jon's ability to meet Sue's emotional needs, not leaving her feeling lonely when he had to travel.

Sue felt that she could travel with Jon on almost every trip. When she couldn't, he would follow the terms of their fifth idea: he would call her several times a day and when he returned they would spend the following weekend together by themselves.

They created a budget, assigning part of Jon's income to pay off their debt. But the added cost of Sue traveling with Jon would prevent them from eliminating it in two years as they would have liked. However, both Jon and Sue were finally enthusiastic about their solution to their problem.

Some marital conflicts are as difficult to solve as Jon's travel problem. But most of them are relatively easy to solve. If you begin with an understanding that a solution cannot be chosen until you have enthusiastic agreement, you will be amazed at how quickly you can find agreement.

To help couples negotiate effectively, I recommend creating a negotiation notebook. Each time there is a problem to resolve, write it out in the notebook with your perspectives and brainstorming ideas. Keep each problem alive, and return to it at least once a week until you've come to an enthusiastic agreement about it.

To help you come to an agreement, leave a margin on the left side of your brainstorming list so that you can rate each other's ideas. Use a scale of -3 to +3, where -3 is an idea you strongly dislike and +3 is one you strongly like. Keep brainstorming until you both rate an idea as a +2 or +3.

There are many conflicts in marriage that should be resolved on a trial basis. You may not know how you would really feel about it until it's been implemented for a week or two. You can be enthusiastic about trying something on a short-term basis if you know that it's not something you must commit yourselves to doing.

If you begin with an understanding that a solution cannot be chosen until you have enthusiastic agreement, you will be amazed at how quickly you can find agreement.

In your notebook, indicate a specific date for implementing the solution. Also include a date to determine if it has actually solved the problem. If your solution doesn't solve the problem, further negotiation may be needed. The notebook helps with memory, follow-through, and accountability, which are often the potential problems to successful negotiation.

At first, to find a solution to their conflicts Jon and Sue had to schedule a time to formally follow the four guidelines I had given them. But the more they practiced, the easier it was for them to come to an enthusiastic agreement, and following the guidelines seemed to come naturally.

Negotiating on the Run

Most marital decisions are not made with calm deliberation. While brainstorming alternatives over a cup of coffee might be the most desirable way to solve problems, in practice, couples need to develop skill in making thoughtful decisions on the run.

So after Jon and Sue had practiced negotiating with the four guidelines I had proposed, I encouraged them to adapt the same guidelines to decisions they made when they were pressed for time. They had a chance to test their skills one Saturday afternoon as they were shopping for new tennis shoes.

As they approached the shoe store they came upon a sidewalk sale—one of Jon's worst nightmares. Sue stopped to look at the clearance tables and spent the next thirty minutes sorting through the bargains.

> *I highly recommend to couples that they learn to say something like, "I'm not very enthusiastic about this situation. Will you discuss this with me?"*

Jon reminded Sue that they had promised the babysitter they would be home by 3:00. Sue quickly called to tell the babysitter that they would be a little late. Jon was not happy with the way the events developed, but he didn't know how to explain it to Sue.

Their problem was that Sue had not asked Jon how he would feel about taking time to look at the bargains on the sidewalk. And Jon had not let Sue know that it was not the babysitter that bothered him; it was her taking the time to shop for bargains. They forgot to use the Policy of Joint Agreement, and as a result they had an unpleasant experience together.

It takes awhile to develop the skill of constantly using the Policy of Joint Agreement to make decisions. I highly recommend to couples that they choose a simple phrase to help express their feelings when negotiation is needed—something like, *I'm not very enthusiastic about this situation. Will you discuss this with me?* This serves as a reminder that no decision should be made without the enthusiastic agreement of both of them. Then, if possible, I encourage them to negotiate "on the run."

Let me show you how this would have worked in Jon and Sue's shopping experience.

Jon sees the endless rows of tables as they enter the mall. He immediately feels anxiety and discomfort because he knows how much Sue loves to shop and how much he hates to wait for her. As Sue starts looking at the tables, Jon could say, *Honey, I'm not very enthusiastic about this situation. Will you discuss this with me?* Sue stops looking at the sale items, and they spend a few minutes considering alternatives. They briefly share their perspectives on the problem without being defensive or demanding and throw out a few possible solutions. They finally agree that Jon will go right to the shoe store, and Sue will meet him there fifteen minutes later. Conflict resolved!

But shouldn't Sue have asked him how he felt about her shopping before she actually started looking at the sale tables? Ideally, yes. But in practice, spouses often assume that they know how each other feels about things, and it often doesn't occur to them to ask. In this example, Sue thought she would spend only a few minutes looking at the sale items and didn't know that Jon would be upset. He had to tell her. But then, once she knew how he felt, the Policy of Joint Agreement would have guided her response. She would have stopped in her tracks and negotiated a resolution to the problem. The four guidelines would then have guided them to a solution that would have saved the afternoon.

Whatever phrase you use to communicate the need for negotiation will probably feel strange at first, as if you are speaking a new language. But there are many advantages to it. The phrase is a gentle reminder to your spouse that you have both agreed to follow the Policy of Joint Agreement, and it keeps you from saying something hurtful out of frustration. By expressing your unhappiness through a sentence you've both agreed to, you trigger a mutual effort to reach an enthusiastic agreement.

The Policy of Joint Agreement Offers Complete Protection

The Policy of Joint Agreement is nothing more than a reminder to be thoughtful. Almost everything one spouse does in some way affects the other spouse. If you have habits that hurt each other, those habits can become excruciatingly painful. You can become your spouse's greatest source of unhappiness unless you deliberately protect your spouse from your thoughtless behavior. So it makes sense to ask, *How do you feel about what I'd like to do?*

If something you want to do is not agreeable to your spouse, the Policy of Joint Agreement offers your spouse protection. Following the policy means that if something you want to do very much would hurt your spouse, you won't do it.

The Policy of Joint Agreement encourages couples to consider each other's happiness to be as important as their own. When one spouse considers his or her own interests so important that he or she tramples over the interests of the other, it's a formula for marital disaster, and yet some of the most well-intentioned couples do it regularly. It's difficult to be thoughtful when it means we won't get what we want.

This policy provides protection from such self-centeredness. It forces a couple to take each other's feelings into account with *every* decision and *every* behavior. By following the policy, a couple makes all of their decisions together, and they avoid final choices until there is an enthusiastic agreement. In this way they build a partnership that will last for life.

The Policy of Joint Agreement Creates a Compatible Lifestyle

Building a marital relationship is like building a house—brick by brick. Each brick is a choice you make about the way you live together. If you follow the Policy of Joint Agreement and make choices that are mutually agreeable, your house will be strong and beautiful. But if some bricks are made by only one of you, those weak bricks will make your whole house an uncomfortable place to live.

When a couple creates a lifestyle that they each enjoy and appreciate, they build compatibility into their marriage.

When couples follow the Policy of Joint Agreement, they gradually throw out all their thoughtless habits and activities and replace them with habits and activities that take each other's feelings into account. That's what compatibility is all about—building a way of life that is comfortable for both spouses. When a couple creates a lifestyle that they each enjoy and appreciate, they build compatibility into their marriage.

Compatibility means that you live in harmony with each other. It means enjoying the lifestyle you created because it is what both of you want and need. Each brick that goes into your house is there because you are both comfortable with it.

Incompatibility, on the other hand, is created when the Policy of Joint Agreement is not followed—when one spouse adds bricks that may be in his or her own best interest but are not in the other's best interest. Incompatibility, therefore, is simply the accumulation of thoughtless habits and activities. The more of them a couple try to tolerate, the more incompatible they become.

Jon and Sue had failed to take each other's feelings into account when making daily decisions. They had built their marriage with independent decisions that created independent lifestyles. Their independence led to an environment that made Sue's affair possible—bricks that threatened to destroy their house.

You Can Be the Greatest Source of Your Spouse's Unhappiness

While it takes a certain amount of planning and effort to be the greatest source of your spouse's happiness, it takes almost no effort to be the greatest source of his or her unhappiness. That's because your instincts will lead you toward all six of the Love Busters I've described, particularly if your Love Bank balances drop into the negative range. And once you let Love Busters invade your marriage, they tend to escalate to such an extent that it becomes unbearable to live with each other.

That's why I focus so much attention on eliminating Love Busters completely. Tolerating them at any level is a formula for disaster. It's like the proverbial camel's nose under the tent—before long, he'll be joining you for dinner.

Jon and Sue learned how to avoid being the source of each other's unhappiness. Granted, they needed to do more than make each other safe, but that first objective was crucial to achieving any of the other objectives. Without safety, any effort to find marital fulfillment is wasted. You cannot expect to be effective at meeting your spouse's emotional needs until you have first learned to protect him or her from your selfish instincts. You can't expect to accumulate love units until you learn to avoid withdrawing them. If you don't eliminate Love Busters, you cannot expect your spouse to love you.

If you have difficulty eliminating your Love Busters—selfish demands, disrespectful judgments, angry outbursts, annoying habits, dishonesty, and independent behavior—I suggest a book I've written that will guide you toward a safer marriage. It is *Love Busters: Protecting Your Marriage from*

Habits That Destroy Romantic Love. In this book, and its accompanying workbook, *Five Steps to Romantic Love,* I help expose the common destructive habits that inflict most marriages. Then I show you how to overcome them so that they no longer ruin the safety of your marriage.

If you need help learning how to negotiate, again, I recommend *Love Busters.* In the second half of this book I explain why negotiation in marriage is so important, and how you can learn to apply the Policy of Joint Agreement to each decision you make in your marriage to create a loving and compatible relationship.

By resolving their conflicts with mutual protection in mind, Sue and Jon were already feeling closer to each other. They had created a plan regarding Jon's traveling that encouraged both of them and they were learning how to negotiate on the run. As a result they felt protected and safe. That, in turn, gave them the courage to become more vulnerable to each other and allow their emotional needs to be met.

───────── ❧ ─────────

Checklist to Avoid Love Bank Withdrawals

Part I: Overcome Love Busters

___ Make a commitment to avoid Love Busters: selfish demands, disrespectful judgments, angry outbursts, annoying habits, dishonesty, and independent behavior (see Memorandum of Agreement, appendix D).

___ Complete the Love Busters Questionnaire (appendix C) and share the information with each other. Remember to create an environment that encourages honesty—protect your spouse from Love Busters when you are being honest and when your spouse is being honest with you.

___ For each Love Buster that your spouse listed, create a plan to eliminate it. Schedule a time for feedback regularly to review your Love Busters until you are Love Buster free.

___ If you need additional help overcoming Love Busters and negotiating with the Policy of Joint Agreement, read *Love Busters* and its accompanying workbook, *Five Steps to Romantic Love*.

Part II: Overcome Dishonesty

Follow the **Policy of Radical Honesty:**

___ Reveal your emotional reactions—both positive and negative—to the events of your life, particularly to your spouse's behavior (Emotional Honesty).

___ Use appropriate complaints such as "I'm bothered by," and "I'd love it if you would [*desired, specific behavior*]," and statements such as "I love it when you [*specific behavior*]" to express negative and positive reactions (Emotional Honesty).

___ Reveal information about your personal history, particularly events that demonstrate personal weakness or failure (Historical Honesty).

___ Complete the Personal History Questionnaire, found in the Questionnaires section of MarriageBuilders.com, to learn more about each other's personal history (Historical Honesty).

____ Reveal information about the events of your day. Provide your spouse with a calendar of your activities, with special emphasis on those that may affect your spouse (Current Honesty).

____ Reveal passwords, email, text messages, phone logs, computer histories, and all other forms of communication. Nothing should be hidden (Current Honesty).

____ Reveal your thoughts and plans regarding future activities and objectives (Future Honesty).

____ Create an environment that encourages honesty by valuing radical honesty.

____ Create an environment that encourages honesty by avoiding demands, disrespect, and anger when your spouse is being honest with you.

____ Avoid demands, disrespect, and anger when you are being honest with your spouse.

____ If there is a threat of physical or emotional abuse from your spouse when you express your honest feelings, separate from your spouse until he or she can guarantee your protection when you are being honest.

Part III: Overcome Independent Behavior

Follow the **Policy of Joint Agreement**:

____ Avoid doing anything until you have come to an enthusiastic agreement.

____ Negotiate with the Policy of Joint Agreement as your goal:

    ____ Guideline 1: Set ground rules to make negotiation pleasant and safe.

    ____ Guideline 2: Identify problem from the perspective of both spouses.

    ____ Guideline 3: Brainstorm solutions with abandon.

    ____ Guideline 4: Choose a solution that is appealing to both spouses.

____ Learn to negotiate on the run:

    ____ Get into the habit of asking *How would you feel?* before making a decision or plan.

____ If one spouse forgets to follow the Policy of Joint Agreement, the other spouse should use a nonthreatening reminder such as, *Honey, I'm not enthusiastic about this situation. Will you discuss this with me?*

____ Use a negotiation notebook to identify problems, document your perspectives, brainstorm possible solutions, and come to an enthusiastic agreement, with dates to implement the solution.

11

Make Deposits, Part I

Meet the Most Important
Emotional Needs

Sue and Jon learned to overcome their instinct to hurt each other when they were upset. And they were upset quite a bit of the time, at least in the beginning of their recovery. If they had not made an effort to avoid blaming each other for the mess they were in, any hope for a successful recovery would have been blown away.

But Sue and Jon committed themselves to avoid selfish demands, disrespectful judgments, and angry outbursts, and they also followed the Policy of Radical Honesty and the Policy of Joint Agreement so that they would avoid making thoughtless decisions.

Most couples recovering from the ravages of an affair should first focus their attention on overcoming Love Busters. Their relationship is usually so fragile that they must be careful not to make matters worse by doing anything that might hurt each other.

But thoughtlessness wasn't the primary factor that led Sue to have an affair. It was Jon's failure to meet her most important emotional needs that had made her particularly vulnerable. So after they learned to eliminate

Love Busters, they were ready to get at the core of their problem: their failure to meet each other's basic needs.

Jon's account in Sue's Love Bank was already empty before she had her affair—she was no longer in love with him. But Jon was still in love with her because she had been meeting his emotional needs. After her affair was over, however, Sue's account in Jon's Love Bank was also in the red. She had not been meeting his emotional needs while they were separated, and the affair itself had caused gigantic Love Bank withdrawals from her account.

So their next goal in their road to recovery was to start making Love Bank deposits—as many and as quickly as possible. But before they could begin, they had to know where to put their effort. They had to identify their own most important emotional needs for each other.

Do you know yourself well enough to list your most important emotional needs? Most people haven't given this much thought, and if forced to make up a list, they would not know where to begin. But it's very important that you understand your emotional needs, not only for your own sake, but for the sake of your spouse. If he or she is going to put time and energy into becoming an expert at meeting those needs, you'd better be sure you've identified the right ones. And it's also important for you to understand your spouse's emotional needs so that you can put your effort in the right place.

When I first realized that the meeting of emotional needs created romantic love, I went to work trying to identify those needs that had the greatest effect. I asked each spouse I counseled to identify what his or her spouse could do to make them the happiest. Their answers helped me identify ten emotional needs so powerful that when certain ones are met by someone of the opposite sex, the feeling of love is created. I listed these ten emotional needs in chapter 3 but I'll repeat the list again here. They are affection, sexual fulfillment, intimate conversation, recreational companionship, honesty and openness, physical attractiveness, financial support, domestic support, family commitment, and admiration. When these needs are met, people experience great pleasure, and when they are not met, they experience great frustration and disappointment.

While almost everyone has these ten needs to some extent, the importance of each need varies greatly from person to person. Some people feel a great deal of pleasure when the need for affection is met. Others don't feel much at all. The same can be said for admiration: some need it greatly, while others don't.

Which needs are the most important to you? Which are the most important to your spouse? If you and your spouse were to choose five out of the ten that you needed the most, it's very likely that the ones you pick will not be exactly the same. They may even be entirely different.

As I said earlier, men and women tend to prioritize these ten needs very differently. Men tend to give highest priority to:

1. Sexual fulfillment
2. Recreational companionship
3. Physical attractiveness
4. Domestic support
5. Admiration

Women, on the other hand, tend to give the highest priority to:

1. Affection
2. Intimate conversation
3. Honesty and openness
4. Financial support
5. Family commitment

Of course, not every man would pick the five needs I listed for men. Nor would every woman pick the five needs listed for women. Some men would include affection and conversation in their top five needs, and some women rank admiration and sexual fulfillment among their most important needs. But on average, I've found that men and women rank these needs the way I listed them.

Since the way men and women tend to prioritize their needs is so different, it's no wonder they have difficulty adjusting in marriage! A man can set out to meet his wife's needs, but he will fail miserably if he assumes that her needs are the same as his. A woman will also fail if she assumes her husband has the same needs as she has.

I have seen this simple error threaten many marriages. A husband and wife fail to meet each other's needs—not because they're selfish or uncaring but because they are ignorant of what those needs are.

She may think that showering him with love notes and affection will please him, because it pleases her. He thinks that he is doing her a big favor by inviting her to play golf, because he would be thrilled by the offer. Both partners think they are valiantly trying to meet each other's needs, but they may be aiming at the wrong target.

So, where should you put your greatest effort so that you can deposit the most love units? Meet each other's *most important* emotional needs.

As I've explained, you are the only one who can identify your most important emotional needs, and your spouse is the best expert on his or her needs. You must ask each other where to put your greatest effort to make each other the happiest.

The ten needs that I focus attention on do not exhaust the list of possible needs. Other needs could be included on your list if they are important to you. This will require you to identify them yourself, from your past experiences. Think about what makes you the happiest when you have it, and the most frustrated when you don't. That will help you identify them. For most of us, though, the ten needs that I listed cover the bases.

List Your Most Important Emotional Needs

I have made it easy for you and your spouse to identify for each other your most important emotional needs. To help you understand your choices, I have described each of the ten most important emotional needs in appendix A. After you have read each description carefully, complete the Emotional Needs Questionnaire I have provided for you in appendix B. Make two enlarged copies of this questionnaire so both you and your spouse can complete one of them.

Remember how I described an emotional need in chapter 3? It is a craving that when satisfied leaves you feeling happy and content, and when unsatisfied leaves you unhappy and frustrated. The word *craving* is an important part of that definition. If you have a craving for any of the possible needs, it should be on your list of most important emotional needs.

When you come to the last page of the questionnaire, where you are asked to rank your needs according to their importance to you, consider the following—if you don't choose sexual fulfillment as a most important need, imagine never having sex with your spouse. If you don't choose affection, imagine your spouse never expressing his or her love for you—no hugs, no kisses, no love notes. If you don't choose financial support, imagine your spouse not earning a dime throughout your life together.

To help you rank your needs, imagine your spouse meeting only one of the ten needs and failing to meet the other nine. Under that condition, which would give you the most satisfaction and the least frustration? Which would deposit the most love units? You should rank that need number 1. Continue this imagining process until you have identified the five emotional needs that mean the most to you.

Before you leave this assignment, give your list of five needs one last look and give special attention to those you didn't include. If all five of the needs you've listed are met by your spouse, will you be happy? If your spouse fails to meet a need that is not included on your list, will it threaten to ruin your marriage? If there is a sixth need that you feel must be included to ensure the success of your marriage, add it to the list. But then let your spouse also add a sixth need to his or her list.

My experience with most couples shows that the higher the ranking, the more effort should be given to meeting that need. In some cases an outstanding job meeting the top two needs is all it takes to deposit enough love units to trigger the feeling of love. If a reasonably good effort is made to meet the other three, it just adds insurance to the Love Bank account. But couples who try to meet all ten needs try to do too much and usually do a poor or mediocre job on all of them. So recovery from an affair depends on each spouse being an expert at meeting the other's top five needs—especially the top two.

Jon and Sue Rank Their Needs

I asked Jon and Sue to do what I just suggested you and your spouse do—identify the most important emotional needs. First, they became familiar with the ten emotional needs by reading a summary of each, and then they both completed the Emotional Needs Questionnaire.

Sue ranked her top five emotional needs as follows:

1. Intimate conversation
2. Affection
3. Admiration
4. Financial support
5. Family commitment

Sue's list helped Jon see why his job had almost ruined their marriage. His financial support was important to her because it met one of her most important emotional needs. But in meeting that need for financial support, he had failed to meet three needs that were more important to her—intimate conversation, affection, and admiration. The time he had taken to earn more money prevented him from meeting those more important emotional needs.

Jon's list of important emotional needs was very different than Sue's. He ranked his needs this way:

1. Sexual fulfillment
2. Physical attractiveness
3. Honesty and openness
4. Domestic support
5. Recreational companionship

Before Sue's affair, Jon had no complaints when it came to his need for sexual fulfillment. Even after Sue began to feel less enthusiastic about making love to Jon, he didn't know about her loss of passion, except for one evening on their eighth wedding anniversary. But after that, she never denied him sex and often approached him when she thought he would like it. Because it was his most important emotional need, in meeting that need Sue continued to deposit more than enough love units for him to be in love with her.

But she did even more for him. She was physically attractive to him, she did a great job managing the home and taking care of their children, and when he had a break in his work schedule, she often joined him in *his* favorite recreational activities. The only need she had failed to meet was his need for honesty and openness. And he didn't know she was being dishonest until her affair had already begun. From Jon's perspective, Sue had been the perfect wife.

But from Sue's perspective, Jon had a lot to learn.

Become an Expert at Meeting Each Other's Most Important Emotional Needs

Most of our happiness in life comes from our relationships with others. That's because we can't meet our most important emotional needs most effectively by ourselves—others must meet them for us. And we usually fall in love with and marry the person we think will do the very best job meeting them.

If you don't agree with what I've just said—if you think that you can meet your own needs—consider again your top five emotional needs. How could you meet them effectively by yourself? Affection, sexual fulfillment, intimate conversation, recreational companionship, physical attractiveness, and so forth. Someone else must meet those very basic needs for you.

Granted, you won't die if those needs go unmet. You'll just be frustrated and lonely. And you'll be missing out on life's greatest pleasures.

Without a doubt, marriage offers happiness and fulfillment when spouses become experts at meeting each other's emotional needs. Being experts simply means that they have made an effort to learn what to do to make each other happy and they do it very well. They do something that's extremely important for each other that they can't do for themselves.

We can't meet our most important emotional needs by ourselves—others must meet them for us.

People take courses regularly to become experts at all sorts of things—typing, computer programming, hairstyling, teaching. And at the beginning, learning any new skill may seem awkward and it usually requires some effort. Take typing, for example. At first it seems very unnatural. You search for every letter. But with practice typing becomes almost effortless and requires very little thought. You just know where the letters are because it has become a well-developed habit.

Habits that meet your spouse's needs develop in the same way. At first they may seem uncomfortable to you, but with practice they become a habit, part of who you are. A good marriage becomes almost effortless when spouses develop habits that meet each other's needs.

When Jon and Sue identified their five most important emotional needs, I asked them to make a trade. Jon would agree to become an expert in meeting Sue's most important emotional needs, and in return Sue would become an expert in meeting Jon's. But my problem with Sue and Jon was not in their *learning* how to meet each other's needs, it was in their *wanting* to meet each other's needs.

With Jon's account so depleted in her Love Bank, Sue did not want to meet Jon's need for sexual fulfillment. And Jon felt the same way about meeting Sue's need for affection and intimate conversation. But if they didn't meet each other's emotional needs, the feeling of love they needed for their marriage would never materialize. Unless they met those needs for each other, there would not be enough love units deposited to trigger the feeling of love in either of them.

A good marriage becomes almost effortless when spouses develop habits that meet each other's needs.

So I asked them to "prime the pump" to get love units flowing. Granted, it would have been almost effortless for them to meet each other's important emotional needs if they had been in love. But if they had waited for love before trying to meet each other's needs, they would still be waiting. My encouragement for both of them to make a trade and try to meet each other's emotional needs right away helped them start depositing those love units that were essential to their marital recovery.

Quality and Quantity

Jon knew how to meet Sue's emotional needs, but because he hadn't been doing it, he was a little rusty. To correct his mistakes and improve his overall performance, he needed feedback from Sue as to how well he was doing. He needed feedback on two aspects of his skill—quality and quantity.

To determine the quality of the way Jon was meeting Sue's needs, he was to ask, *Are you satisfied with the way I am meeting this need?*

If the answer was *no*, he would then ask, *How would you like me to meet this need?* Sue's response was to be specific and offer a positive suggestion. She was to avoid only saying, *I don't like it when you do ____.* Instead, she was to say, *I'd love it if you would do____, or I'd prefer it if you would do____.* A positive suggestion offers direction and encouragement.

To determine whether the quantity of need fulfillment was adequate, Jon was to ask Sue, *Do I meet this need for you often enough?*

If Sue's answer was *no*, then he was to ask, *How often would you like me to meet this need?* If she wanted more time talking with him or if she wanted him to show admiration for her more often or if she wanted more affection, he would then try to accommodate her wishes.

When you learn to meet each other's emotional needs, you will need to satisfy both the quality and quantity requirements to make your spouse happy. Quantity is fairly easy to understand, because your spouse will tell you how often and how much he or she wants the need met. But quality is more difficult to communicate. Sometimes even the one with the need doesn't understand exactly what's missing.

Not surprisingly Sue asked for more conversation, and that was very encouraging to Jon. It meant that she wanted him to deposit more love units, and the more he deposited, the closer he came to reaching her romantic love threshold. Sue didn't love him yet, but her willingness to let him meet her emotional needs meant that it was only a matter of time before they would have a terrific marriage.

Meet Each Other's Needs in Ways That Are Mutually Enjoyable

When you ask each other to improve skills in need fulfillment, remember the four steps for negotiation that I discussed in chapter 10. The most important step is the first one, where you guarantee each other a safe and pleasant negotiating environment. If one of you becomes negative or unpleasant during your discussion, take a break and get back to your negotiations at a time when you can guarantee that the guidelines will be followed.

You should also remember to follow the Policy of Joint Agreement as you develop your new skills. There will be many effective ways to meet each other's emotional needs. Some methods will be enjoyable for you to follow, and others may be very unpleasant. Because you are trying very hard to move toward marital recovery, you may be tempted to meet each other's needs at all costs. But I strongly advise you to avoid this.

You should have an understanding that you will meet each other's needs only in ways that are enjoyable for both of you. Never expect the other person to suffer or sacrifice so that your need can be met. But since it is usually somewhat uncomfortable at first to form a new habit, don't confuse the discomfort of learning something new with a behavior that will always be unpleasant to you. In other words, give a new habit a chance to become comfortable before you abandon it.

> *Never expect the other person to suffer or sacrifice so that your need can be met.*

The topics of Sue and Jon's conversation had to be interesting to both of them. The recreational activities they chose had to be mutually enjoyable. They were willing to experiment with conversation and recreation. They tried different topics of conversation for a while and engaged in various recreational activities to see how they would feel about them.

But in the area of sexual fulfillment, they had a special problem. Before their separation, Sue had been in the habit of making love to Jon out of duty. Now that they were together again, she was still uncomfortable making love. Besides, being out of love with Jon made lovemaking particularly unappealing to her.

I suggested that they experiment with sex the same way they experimented with conversation and recreation. They had to try to find a way to make love that would satisfy Jon, yet still be comfortable for Sue.

Granted, at first, it was not exactly what Jon had in mind. He knew how passionate Sue could be, and their lovemaking certainly lacked passion as far as he was concerned. But as Jon deposited more and more love units into Sue's Love Bank, he came closer and closer to triggering her love for him. It was only a matter of time before her feeling of love would be restored and, along with it, all the passion he remembered.

You Can Be the Source of Your Spouse's Greatest Happiness

You married each other because you were in love. And you were in love because you were meeting each other's most important emotional needs—you were a source of each other's greatest happiness.

Since you have been married, you may have squandered your opportunity to be each other's source of greatest happiness. But it can be recovered by going back to what you did before you were married—making it your mission to meet each other's most important emotional needs.

You can be each other's greatest source of happiness. In fact this *must* be your goal if you want to have a successful marriage. You have given each other the opportunity to care in a way that no one else can care for you. And if you and your spouse don't use that opportunity, you will both feel that something important is missing.

An important part of learning to be an expert in meeting each other's important emotional needs is the respect you give to each other every step of the way.

First, you must identify each other's needs, and when you discover them you must be respectful regarding the needs themselves. It's tempting for all of us to be disrespectful of what we don't need ourselves. When our spouse has needs that are different than ours, which is almost always the case, we may believe that the needs are unnecessary or even wrong. In fact, every emotional need I've listed can be treated disrespectfully by a spouse who doesn't have as great a need. The need for affection can be viewed by those without that need as a sign of insecurity. A spouse with a need for sexual fulfillment can be criticized as being "oversexed." Those who believe this try to convince a spouse that he or she should learn not to have that need, or at least not to indulge it. The outcome, of course, it that the need is not met, and the spouse's opportunity to deposit love units is lost.

You must be each other's greatest source of happiness if you want to have a successful marriage.

If you want to be the source of your spouse's greatest happiness, you must begin by knowing what will create the greatest happiness for your spouse. Accept what you discover—an honest expression of your spouse's needs. If you don't, you will waste your time trying to meet needs that are of less importance to him or her.

After you identify each other's emotional needs, you must be respectful in the way you teach each other to become experts in meeting them. Feedback from your spouse as to how you are doing at meeting his or her emotional needs is absolutely essential in your becoming an expert. But if you want your spouse to be willing to give you feedback, you must receive it respectfully. A response that is defensive and even angry will end your spouse's willingness to help you become skilled. And respect is also necessary in the way feedback is expressed. Every time you discuss your skill development, Love Busters are in the wings ready to enter. And if you let them on stage, they will destroy the show. So remember to keep your conversation safe and pleasant whenever you discuss the way you meet each other's needs.

Knowing how to meet each other's emotional needs was not a problem for Jon and Sue. But I've counseled many spouses who have never learned those important marital skills. These spouses must train themselves to become experts in conversation or showing admiration or affection. If you have difficulty becoming experts in meeting each other's most important emotional needs, I suggest that you both read my book, *His Needs, Her Needs: Building an Affair-Proof Marriage*. That book and its accompanying workbook, *Five Steps to Romantic Love*, will provide guidance that goes beyond what has been offered here.

Sue and Jon could remember what it had been like to be the source of each other's greatest happiness before the tragedy of the affair. But they didn't think they could completely recover from all of the resentment and hopelessness they were feeling. Deep down, they thought that their bad experiences would sentence them to a marriage that would never quite recover.

But they were wrong. They had new tools at their disposal that would not only help them recover the best feelings they ever had for each other, but move them beyond that point. Their skills in meeting each other's needs would become unprecedented in their marriage. They still had a lot to learn but they were on their way toward creating a marriage that was more fulfilling than anything they could have ever imagined. They were on their way to becoming the source of each other's greatest happiness.

12

Make Deposits, Part II

Take Time for Undivided Attention

*B*y now, you should be fairly familiar with the Love Bank and how it affects the way we feel about people. Those whose accounts have high positive balances are attractive to us—we want them to spend time with us so that they can make more deposits. But we find those who have negative balances to be repulsive—we want to avoid them and their tendency to make withdrawals.

When I began counseling Jon and Sue for recovery, both of their accounts in each other's Love Banks were in negative territory. They were willing to avoid Love Busters, which prevented further withdrawals. But their negative accounts made them dislike each other. Their emotions encouraged them to avoid each other whenever possible so they resisted spending much time with each other. That made my job much more difficult, because they had to be together if they were to meet each other's important emotional needs.

Of course, before Sue married Jon, spending time with him was never a problem—she spent most of her free time with him. After they started dating, she made their time together one of her highest priorities. Whenever her friends invited her somewhere, she would first check with Jon to see if he was busy at that time. On some occasions she even broke dates with her friends if Jon found time to be with her.

Jon also made spending time with Sue his highest priority. Friends and activities that he had enjoyed prior to meeting Sue were abandoned because he had found a much more fulfilling relationship. He certainly didn't miss any of them, because he loved being with Sue.

When they were together, which was almost every day, they usually gave each other their undivided attention. On days that they couldn't be together, they talked to each other on the phone, sometimes for hours. They spent about fifteen to twenty-five hours together each week, including time on the phone. But they weren't counting. They took whatever opportunities there were to be together, and it just turned out to be that much time.

After Jon and Sue were married, however, the quality of their time together suffered. While they were with each other more often, they spent less time giving each other their undivided attention. When they came home from work, they talked to each other as Sue prepared dinner and Jon helped pick things up around the apartment. They talked during dinner and they did the dishes together. But after dinner they watched television and sometimes barely said a word to each other. Some evenings Sue would read a book while Jon watched a sporting event. They usually went to bed at the same time and some evenings they made love. But even then they did not say much to each other.

Prior to marriage, when watching television, Jon and Sue would often be so affectionate that they didn't pay any attention to the program. But after marriage, they were rarely affectionate while watching TV. They usually sat in separate chairs, and sometimes watched in different rooms so that they could each see a favorite program.

Another important change after marriage was dating. Before marriage, Jon and Sue went out often—to dinner, a movie, a sporting event, or just on a walk. Sue looked forward to being with Jon but she also looked forward to going out. She liked dating Jon because they always did something fun together. After marriage they spent a lot of time just sitting at home watching TV.

When their children arrived, they went out even less often. And they talked to each other less. The children were a major distraction, and the responsibilities kept them both hopping. That was when Jon and Sue decided that he needed to put his career into high gear so that they could provide their children with a wonderful lifestyle. And that gave them even less time to be with each other.

Neither Jon nor Sue realized that after they married their time together had ceased being a high priority. In fact almost everything else in their lives had become more important than their time together. Looking back, Jon and Sue could see how they had drifted apart. Jon was at work and away from his family almost seventy hours each week. And when he was home, he was exhausted. Sue spent her days focused on her children, her work, and her community activities. Although she missed having Jon at home, she found her life too busy to worry much about it.

Now, even though Jon and Sue were committed to marital recovery, they found it difficult to schedule time to be together. They understood the importance of it, but to actually schedule their time turned out to be one of their most difficult assignments. They tried to talk me out of the amount of time I recommended—at least fifteen hours each week. They began by trying to convince me that it was impossible. Then they went on to the argument that it was impractical. But in the end, Jon and Sue agreed that without a substantial amount of time together, they would not be able to meet each other's emotional needs and recreate the love they once had for each other. They agreed to follow my Policy of Undivided Attention.

The Policy of Undivided Attention

Give undivided attention to your spouse a minimum of fifteen hours each week, meeting each other's emotional needs of affection, sexual fulfillment, intimate conversation, and recreational companionship.

The purpose of the Policy of Undivided Attention is to guarantee enough time each week to meet the four most intimate emotional needs, because they are usually the ones that make the most massive Love Bank deposits. For most men, it's sexual fulfillment and recreational companionship that are identified as their top two emotional needs, and for most women it's affection and intimate conversation that lead their list. By setting aside time to meet all four of those needs every week, a husband and wife keep their Love Banks overflowing.

To help Jon and Sue fully understand the Policy of Undivided Attention and how it was to be applied as they made their weekly schedules, I told them about its three parts: privacy, objectives, and amount.

Privacy: *The time you plan to be together should not include children, relatives, or friends. Establish privacy so that you are able to give each other your undivided attention.*

It is essential that, as a couple, you spend time with each other alone. When you have time alone, you have a much greater opportunity to meet emotional needs that require undivided attention. Without privacy, undivided attention is almost impossible, and without undivided attention, you are not likely to meet some of each other's most intimate emotional needs.

First, I recommend that you learn to be together without your children. Many couples don't think children interfere with their privacy. To them, an evening with their children *is* privacy. Of course, they know they can't make love with children around. But I believe that the presence of children prevents much more than lovemaking. When children are present, they interfere with the affection and intimate conversation that are desperately needed in marriage.

Second, I recommend that friends and relatives not be present during your time together. This may mean that after everything has been scheduled, there's no time left over for friends and relatives. If that's the case, you're too busy, but at least you won't be sacrificing your love for each other.

Third, I recommend that you understand what giving undivided attention means. Remember, it's what you did while dating. There's no way you would have been married if you had ignored each other on dates. You looked at each other when you were talking, you were interested in the conversation, and there was little to distract you. This is the undivided attention you must give each other now.

When you are seeing a movie together, you do not give each other undivided attention. It's the same with television or sporting events. I'm not saying that you should not do these things together, but the time you spend at them doesn't count toward fulfilling the time for undivided attention. That time is very clearly defined—it's the time you pay *close* attention to each other.

Jon and Sue recognized where they had gone wrong on the few dates they had with each other after being married. Jon would bring his cell phone along and become distracted by a business call while they were having dinner together. This left Sue feeling that she was low on his list of priorities. Whoever was on the other end of the telephone seemed to be much more important to Jon than she was.

Sue could also see how she had sabotaged their time together by inviting their children or another couple to join them at the last minute. Jon had wanted to be alone with Sue, but she had often insisted on including others on their nights out. Now they both agreed to invite others on their dates *only after* they had spent enough time together by themselves.

Jon and Sue were committed to being alone with each other. But what should they do with this time? The second part of the Policy of Undivided Attention deals with objectives.

Objectives: *During the time you are together, create activities that will meet the emotional needs of affection, sexual fulfillment, intimate conversation, and recreational companionship.*

Time is valuable and should be used wisely. So when a couple schedules time for undivided attention, they should know precisely what they hope to accomplish with that time. Their goal should be to deposit as many love units as possible into each other's Love Bank. And the way to deposit the most love units is to meet each other's most important emotional needs.

Some important emotional needs can be met without undivided attention. For example, domestic support, family commitment, and financial support can be met without a spouse even being present. However, there are some emotional needs that can be met only with undivided attention. The most obvious one is sexual fulfillment. But affection, intimate conversation, and recreational companionship are also best met in marriage with undivided attention.

For most men, sexual fulfillment and recreational companionship are among their top five emotional needs, and they are usually their top two. For most women, affection and intimate conversation are their top two emotional needs. So when all four are met on a date, men and women alike call it romance. That combination usually deposits the most love units possible for both spouses. My advice, then, is to try to meet all four of these needs when you schedule time for undivided attention.

But after marriage, spouses are tempted to take shortcuts. They try to have their spouse meet their own needs without meeting the needs of their spouse. They have plenty of energy and time to have their own needs met, but find themselves too tired or too busy to meet their spouse's needs. Women may want their husbands to be affectionate and to talk to them without necessarily offering recreational companionship and sexual fulfillment in return. Men, on the other hand, may want their wives to meet their needs for sexual fulfillment and recreational companionship without offering affection and intimate conversation in return. Neither strategy works very well. Women usually resent having sex without affection and intimate conversation first, and men usually resent being attentive and affectionate when there's no hope for sex and recreation. By combining the four needs into a single event, however, both spouses have their needs met and enjoy their time together.

If time is not set aside to meet all four needs, it is assumed that they can be met on the run—with no planning needed. A husband assumes that when he is in bed with his wife at the end of a day, sex should be there for the taking. His wife goes to bed dreading a possible ambush each night, while her husband fears rejection. A wife, on the other hand, assumes that her husband should drop whatever he's doing to be affectionate or talk with her whenever she feels the need. When these four needs are not met together, both spouses feel used and neglected.

The right way to meet all four emotional needs is to schedule enough time to meet them all.

The right way to meet all four emotional needs is to schedule enough time to meet them all. Trying to squeeze meeting these needs into an existing schedule is like buying shoes that are too small—the pain will be excruciating. You will simply not have enough time to do it right.

When you schedule time for undivided attention, don't forget some of the other important emotional needs that can also be met during that time together, such as the needs for physical attractiveness, honesty and openness, and admiration. When dating, you tried to present yourselves as attractively as possible to each other, gave information about yourselves freely and completely, and complimented each other whenever possible. Take a lesson from your courtship days and make sure that when you spend time together for undivided attention, you look your very best, you're completely honest, and you express how much you value each other.

Keeping in mind the importance of meeting so many needs when you give each other your undivided attention, how much time should you schedule? That's what the third part of the Policy of Undivided Attention helps determine.

Amount: *The number of hours scheduled each week for undivided attention should reflect the quality of your marriage. If your marriage is satisfying to you and your spouse, schedule fifteen hours each week for your undivided attention. But if you suffer marital dissatisfaction, plan more time at first, until marital satisfaction is achieved.*

How much time do you need to sustain the feeling of romantic love? Believe it or not, there really is an answer to this question and it depends on the health of a marriage. If a couple is deeply in love with each other and find that their marital needs are being met, I have found that about fifteen hours each week of undivided attention is usually enough to sustain romantic love. But it's the least amount of time necessary. If you are in love with each other and your emotional needs are being met by each other, you're either newly married or you have already been giving each other fifteen hours a week of your undivided attention.

In Jon and Sue's case, they knew that I wanted them to spend a minimum of fifteen hours a week together for undivided attention. But for the first few weeks, I suggested that they spend even more time together. In fact, I recommended that Jon take some time off from work so that they could take a vacation together—just the two of them.

When I apply the fifteen-hour principle to marriages, I usually recommend that there is enough time scheduled to meet all four emotional needs. I've found that if a couple schedule four three- to four-hour dates during the week, they are able to do it without being rushed. But at the same time, a couple should be emotionally connected on almost a daily basis to sustain their love for each other. So brief conversations and acts of affection throughout the day are also highly recommended.

The reason I have so much difficulty getting couples to spend time alone together is that when I first see them for counseling, they're not in love. Their relationship doesn't do anything for them, and the time spent with each other seems like a total waste. But when they spend time together, they learn to recreate the experiences that first met each other's emotional needs. And that time is spent redepositing love units into Love Bank accounts that are seriously overdrawn. Eventually, enough love units are deposited to trigger the feeling of love. That makes this time together much more appealing.

But without time to make Love Bank deposits, a couple has little hope of restoring the love they once had for each other. In fact for them, fifteen hours a week may not be enough. Jumpstarting their relationship may require twenty-five or thirty hours a week of undivided attention. This is why I recommended a vacation for Jon and Sue. It gave them extra time at the beginning of recovery to deposit more love units.

When I mention trips and scheduling fifteen hours of time to give each other undivided attention, some couples find it unrealistic due to financial restrictions. But even those who have a limited budget can schedule time together, it just means being creative. Here are a few suggestions that might help.

- *Babysitting co-op.* One major roadblock for many is the cost of baby-sitting, added to the cost of going out. Childcare is expensive these days. To help couples with this financial constraint, I have recommended joining or forming a babysitting co-op in your community or church. Another less formal idea is to simply ask friends with children if they would join in a weekly child swap—you watch their children one evening each week in exchange for their watching your children one evening.

- *Rearrange your budget priorities.* Many couples I have counseled don't think they have enough money for weekend escapes together. Jon and Sue certainly felt that way. They were in trouble financially. But as they came to understand the importance of their time together, they were able to create a budget that included enough money each month to go out a few evenings and occasionally to get away for weekends. The purpose of a budget is to be sure you have enough money available to achieve your life's objectives, and meeting important emotional needs in marriage should be your highest priority.

- *Be creative.* Meeting each other's important emotional needs doesn't have to be expensive. There are many ways you can get alone with each other to talk, be affectionate, be together recreationally, and make love without having to spend much money. Don't avoid going out together just because money is tight. Go out regularly but find things to do that you can afford.

Scheduling Time for Undivided Attention

Kevin and Lee, the couple we met in chapter 5, were off to a good start when it came to taking time for undivided attention. They began exercising together three times a week, having lunch together almost every day, and talking on the phone several times during the day. They also scheduled Saturday night as their weekly date night. When they charted their time together, they consistently spent more than twenty hours each week with each other. Prior to Kevin's affair, they had given each other undivided attention less than an hour each week.

As soon as Kevin had recovered from the symptoms of withdrawal, his time with Lee met his emotional needs and deposited hundreds of love units in Lee's account. It wasn't long before he was in love with Lee again, and that made their time together even more enjoyable for him. Lee was also feeling more fulfilled than she had in years. Although Kevin's affair was an unwelcome trauma, she confessed to me that it shocked them out of their apathy. It forced them to create a new lifestyle that provided a fulfilling marriage.

Isn't it a shame that it took an affair to bring Kevin and Lee to their senses? Of course, Lee had not suffered anything close to what Jon suffered as a result of Sue's affair. But even Jon felt that her affair may have been necessary to bring him to a full understanding of how important it was to set aside time to meet Sue's emotional needs. And yet if Sue and Jon had not scheduled time to be alone with each other, even the lessons of the affair may have been all for nothing.

A couple's love for each other cannot be created or sustained without time for undivided attention. And unless you schedule time to meet each other's emotional needs, it won't get done. As I mentioned earlier, setting aside time to give each other undivided attention is one of the most difficult assignments I can give because the pressures of life usually crowd out the time it takes to sustain romantic love.

> *A couple's love for each other cannot be created or sustained without time for undivided attention.*

Jon and Sue brought their day planners to their session each week. We sat down and scheduled at least fifteen hours a week when they could give each other undivided attention. They decided what to do during those times and wrote it in. They also set aside a time at the end of each week to evaluate how well they did. Eventually they did the scheduling themselves. Jon and Sue got into a habit of getting together every Sunday afternoon at 3:00 and scheduling their time for the week to come.

Since we are creatures of habit, I recommend that you schedule the same hours to be alone with your spouse each week. If you keep the same schedule, it will be easier to follow the Policy of Undivided Attention.

The total amount of time you spend together doesn't necessarily affect the way you feel about each other in the week that the time is spent. It has more effect on the way you're going to feel about each other in future weeks. You are building your Love Bank accounts when you spend enjoyable time together, and the account must build before you feel the effect.

> *I recommend that you schedule the same hours to be alone with your spouse each week.*

When Jon and Sue first started spending time together, their Love Bank accounts were in the red. Their emotional reactions to their negative balances made it difficult to enjoy each other's company. So at first, they complained that their time together was uncomfortable and they had trouble finding things to talk about. But their efforts to make their time together enjoyable eventually paid off. They built their Love Bank accounts to a point where they brought out the very best in each other, and conversation became almost effortless.

Many couples mention that they see a noticeable improvement once they start scheduling time to be together. They also feel a noticeable irritability, resentment, and loneliness when time together is not set as a priority and they miss a week. Jon and Sue were very familiar with the hurtful feelings associated with their relationship having low priority. So to avoid its recurrence, they made a commitment to each other that they would make their time for undivided attention their very highest priority. Nothing would get in its way.

Recreational Companionship

Jon and Sue discovered that they must do more than just schedule time to be together and give each other undivided attention. They had to make their time together the most enjoyable time of their week. But what should they do that they would both enjoy? Many activities that they enjoyed in their twenties were no longer fun in their thirties. Or an activity that Jon still enjoyed was no longer enjoyable to Sue.

Couples often make the fatal mistake of going their separate ways when an activity becomes boring to one of the spouses.

Couples often make the fatal mistake of going their separate ways when an activity becomes boring to one of the spouses. After all, they reason, why make one spouse sacrifice an enjoyable activity just to accommodate the other? If one spouse has become skilled playing golf, for example, why give it up just because the other spouse has lost interest in the sport?

The answers to those questions depend on the importance of love in your marriage. If the love you desire for each other is more important than your leisure activities, then you must spend your most enjoyable time with each other, and that time must be mutually enjoyable.

But if your leisure activities are more important than your love, then you will pursue your favorite activities independently of each other. If that's your choice, and if you don't spend your most enjoyable time together, you risk losing your emotional bond and your love for each other. If you choose to spend your most enjoyable leisure time apart, you not only miss an opportunity to build mutual love, but if the activity is with someone of the opposite sex, you risk having an affair. Who should get the Love Bank credits when you are enjoying yourself the most, your spouse or someone else?

It's extremely important to be each other's best friend throughout life. You do that by making each other a part of every enjoyable activity you have. If it's fun to do, your spouse should do it with you. If your spouse doesn't enjoy doing it, give it up. Whatever activity you choose—jogging, bicycling, golfing—be sure your spouse wants to do it, too. Don't develop skills in an activity that your spouse does not enjoy.

One of the quickest ways to become bored with each other is to have more interesting things to do when you are apart. Eliminate that destructive possibility by deliberately spending your most enjoyable moments with each other. Spend as much of your leisure time together as possible and try to use that time to also meet the emotional needs of affection, intimate conversation, and sexual fulfillment. Not only is spending leisure time together one of the best ways to build your relationship, but it ensures that the most interesting and enjoyable parts of your life are experienced together.

13

Make Deposits, Part III

Protect Your Love Bank
from Outside Threats

*T*he feeling of romantic love is extremely important in marriage. It not only provides the passion that you expect from each other, but it also helps make you eager to meet each other's emotional needs. Everything I've been advising you to do in your marriage is much easier when you're in love. The feeling of love makes these actions seem almost instinctive.

But if you were to fall in love with someone else, all of those instincts that should be directed toward your spouse become directed to that someone else. The logical bond between two who have committed themselves to care for each other and their children throughout life is replaced by an irrational bond with someone who cannot possibly provide long-term happiness and security. Romantic love in marriage supports the sensible goal of raising a family with security; romantic love outside of marriage supports the absurd goal of ruining everything a family values.

I call the reasoning power of those having an affair "the fog." They seem incapable of understanding the seriousness of their mistake and the suffering they are causing themselves and others. Romantic love can do that to you. In marriage, romantic love aids our intelligence and helps us achieve some of our most valuable objectives. Outside of marriage, it turns us into fools.

With the risk of falling in love with someone other than your spouse in mind, it's imperative that you guard your Love Bank from outside intruders. The feeling of love is triggered when someone of the opposite sex has deposited enough love units in your Love Bank to breach the romantic love threshold. *How can someone do that?* you may ask. By now you should know the answer. All that's required is that the person meet one of your most important emotional needs. If you give someone other than your spouse the opportunity to make you particularly happy and fulfilled, you'll find yourself in the fog. Everything in you will encourage you to spend more time with this person who makes you feel so good, even if it's a threat to your spouse, your children, your values, your livelihood, your health, and everything else important to you.

That's why I leave you with one more policy—an insurance policy—to protect your Love Banks from outside threats.

The Policy of Exclusivity
Meet each other's most important emotional needs exclusively.

At the time of your wedding, you probably vowed to be faithful to each other—to have an exclusive sexual relationship. You are now fully aware of the suffering that breaking that vow can cause. But most affairs do not begin with sex. They begin when other important emotional needs are met that trigger romantic love—and that leads to sex. My point is that anything someone does that can trigger your feeling of love for them is a danger to your marriage.

So to avoid finding yourself in love with someone else, it's important to guard your Love Bank. This also includes being cautious about how you affect Love Banks outside of your marriage.

Precautions to Protect Your Love Bank from Outside Threats

When it comes to meeting certain emotional needs exclusively, I'm not suggesting that you live as hermits, keeping yourselves away from all outside contact with those of the opposite sex. But as with your agreement to meet each other's sexual need exclusively, you should treat the meeting of other highly charged emotional needs in the same way. You should simply make it difficult for those of the opposite sex to make large deposits into your Love Banks and for you to make large deposits into theirs.

To help you set your boundaries, these are the seven precautions I highly recommend that will help you guard your Love Bank.

1. Affection is the symbolic expression of care and is a powerful emotional need, especially for women. When a man communicates his concern for the problems she faces and his willingness to be there for her when she needs him, she can fall in love with him. Hugs, cards, gifts, and other gestures of kindness that are not intended to trigger romantic feelings can innocently do just that when offered. So I caution husbands to express their greatest affection to their wives and limit it to other women.

Even if a wife expresses comfort in the way her husband shows care for other women, I still recommend caution. But if a wife is uncomfortable with her husband's affection toward other women and he continues to do it, he's violating the Policy of Joint Agreement. He is ignoring her feelings so that he can do what he pleases. When a wife complains to her husband that his affectionate nature can send the wrong message, she's right. And if he ignores that complaint, he not only offends her but also creates the conditions for an affair.

A spouse should not only avoid being affectionate with those of the opposite sex, but should also resist receiving affection from others. When someone of the opposite sex communicates his or her willingness to come to the rescue when needed, red flags should be waving. Granted, when a wife's marriage is in trouble, expressions of care can be very uplifting. It's good to know someone cares when your spouse doesn't seem to show much interest. But at this time of vulnerability, she should get help from another woman or a professional marriage counselor who can provide a solution to her marital problems.

2. Almost all couples begin their marriage with a vow to be sexually faithful. They understand the risks of infidelity. But they don't necessarily understand how exclusive their sex should be. So I've given couples I've counseled a rule to follow that maximizes the sexual pleasure they provide each other and minimizes the risk of an affair: *Engage in every sexual act or experience with your spouse and only with your spouse.*

This rule that limits all forms of sex to marriage is based on what psychologists call the contrast effect: when comparing two experiences, the most enjoyable will make the other seem boring. So when a spouse tells me that sex has become boring, I suspect competing forms of sex. Pornography, strip clubs, masturbation, and other forms of nonmarital sex are often the culprit. If you want marital sex to be the most enjoyable, it should not compete with other sexual experiences.

But sexual exclusivity requires sexual cooperation. If you are each other's exclusive sex partners, you should provide the quality and quantity of sex that leaves neither of you frustrated. Granted, if you are not in love and have a lower need for sexual fulfillment, this may be a particularly difficult assignment. As with all emotional needs, however, if you engage in lovemaking in as mutually enjoyable a way as possible, Love Bank deposits will be made. Eventually, when you have restored your love for each other, it will become almost instinctive.

3. Intimate conversation is the communication of personal topics such as your hopes and dreams, the struggles you have in life, your victories and defeats—whatever it is that expresses your deepest thoughts and feelings. Such conversation is very important to almost everyone, but especially to women. When they exchange intimate details of their lives with someone of the opposite sex, massive Love Bank deposits are made. That's why it's an essential ingredient in marriage.

But what if the husband refuses to talk? Where does she go to relieve her craving for intimate conversation? When a male friend asks the innocent question, *How are you feeling?*, it's so easy to answer the question honestly. And that intimate conversation would be so fulfilling that she'd be likely to fall in love with the man who is truly interested in knowing the answer.

Most affairs begin with intimate conversation. It usually begins without any romantic intentions, but the Love Bank doesn't consider intent—it only considers a person's account balance. Once it reaches the romantic love threshold, it triggers romantic love for the wrong person. And that's a tragic outcome for a marriage.

It's hard to convince spouses who have never experienced an affair to avoid intimate conversation with those of the opposite sex. They don't see the risk. But those who have been through an affair, like you, should know that it's too dangerous to ignore.

This precaution is especially true for topics about marital problems. When the question *how are you feeling* is answered with a flood of tears and an expression of deep disappointment in marriage, the other person is highly motivated to come to the rescue: *I'll be there to help when your husband neglects you or treats you badly.* That's how Greg managed to become such an essential part of Sue's life—he rescued her.

Social networks over the internet are becoming increasingly popular, and are also becoming one of the most common breeding grounds for infidelity. It makes sense, because through these networks people exchange intimate details about themselves and receive support from each other for the problems they face. It's no wonder that so many men and women fall in love with a friend that they know only through a social network. So it isn't only face-to-face conversations that should be guarded. All correspondence that reveals your personal problems to someone of the opposite sex should be avoided.

4. Spend most of your recreational time either alone or with your spouse, so that when you are having a good time, your spouse is right there enjoying it with you. Avoid recreational activities with someone of the opposite sex who could build Love Bank balances by simply being with you when you're having fun.

I have found that exercising together can be one of the fastest ways to build Love Bank balances in marriage. There are a host of physiological reasons why so many love units are deposited during a workout. So for that same reason, you should avoid exercising with someone else of the opposite sex. The gym is a very common place for affairs to begin.

5. If someone of the opposite sex ever tells you that he or she finds you attractive, thank that person for the compliment but don't return it. Also, tell your spouse about the compliment. In general, avoid telling anyone of the opposite sex, other than your spouse, that you feel he or she is attractive. If your feelings of attraction are ever revealed, avoid seeing or talking to that person.

6. Avoid contact with all past lovers. High school and college reunions, weddings, and even funerals are notorious places for breaking this precaution. If one of these events must be attended, have your spouse by your side at all times. While occasional contact with an ex-spouse is often impossible

to avoid, I recommend that your spouse deal primarily with the ex-spouse for parenting issues.

7. Even though you take all of the precautions I've recommended, and others besides, it's possible for someone to make enough Love Bank deposits to breach your romantic love threshold. If you ever find yourself infatuated with someone other than your spouse, for whatever reasons, don't walk away—run! Avoid that person at all costs.

If that ever happens to you, the first person to know about it should be your spouse. Then plan with your spouse how you will break off contact with that person. It's often a friend or even a relative of your spouse that has the opportunity to make that many Love Bank deposits, and breaking off contact with that person is not easy to do. I can't tell you how many "best friends" of a spouse have turned out to be the betrayer. But it makes sense that a friend or relative would be in the best position to make Love Bank deposits. Regardless of who it is, have nothing to do with him or her, even if it means quitting your job, leaving your church, or moving from your neighborhood. And, above all, don't ever tell him or her how you feel.

These precautions may seem unreasonably constraining and strict to you. But they are the precautions that I've followed throughout my entire married life, and I don't feel the least bit unhappy because they've helped me avoid an affair. That's certainly worth every precaution I've taken. It's like avoiding anything that creates a high risk—like smoking. Why raise the risk of lung or throat cancer? Whatever immediate pleasure a person might experience isn't to be compared with the long, slow death that many smokers are forced to endure.

Those who have not followed these precautions until they've had an affair usually realize their value and wish that they had followed them sooner. But those who fail to see their value, and are unwilling to take these precautions, will continue to be at risk for future pain and loss.

These suggestions are only a minor inconvenience when compared to the disaster of infidelity. And they do more than prevent an affair—they also build a stronger emotional bond in the marriage. They're well worth taking.

❧

Checklist to Make Love Bank Deposits

Part I: Meet the Most Important Emotional Needs

1. Identify your most important emotional needs:

    ___ Read about the ten most important emotional needs in appendix A.

    ___ Make two enlarged copies of the Emotional Needs Questionnaire, in appendix B, one for you and one for your spouse.

    ___ Complete the questionnaire and rank your top five emotional needs according to their importance.

2. Become an expert at meeting your spouse's most important emotional needs:

    ___ Agree to become an expert at meeting each other's top five emotional needs.

    ___ List these needs on the Memorandum of Agreement (appendix D).

    ___ Discover how to meet each other's emotional needs, regarding quantity and quality ("How often would you like that need met?" and "How would you like me to meet your need?").

    ___ When giving feedback on quality and quantity, offer specific and positive suggestions ("I'd love it if you would do ___.") instead of only negative feedback.

    ___ Allow time for new behavior that meets emotional needs to first become comfortable and then become enjoyable.

    ___ Meet each other's needs in ways that are mutually enjoyable. Never expect your spouse to suffer.

    ___ Continue to give feedback to your spouse regarding your most important emotional needs. Schedule a time for feedback regularly to review the five needs until you are both meeting them.

    ___ Read *His Needs, Her Needs* and use its accompanying workbook, *Five Steps to Romantic Love*, if you need help learning how to become an expert in meeting your spouse's important emotional needs.

Part II: Take Time for Undivided Attention

Follow the **Policy of Undivided Attention**:

1. Privacy:

____ Plan your time together to be without children, relatives, or friends.

____ Avoid other distractions so that you can give each other your undivided attention.

2. Objectives:

____ Create activities that will meet the emotional needs of affection, sexual fulfillment, intimate conversation, and recreational companionship when you schedule your time together.

____ Choose recreational activities that are mutually enjoyable.

3. Amount:

____ Schedule at least fifteen hours for undivided attention each week. Choose a time each week to make that schedule.

____ Overcome financial obstacles that prevent giving each other undivided attention:

____ Join or start a babysitting co-op.

____ Rearrange your budget priorities.

____ Be creative and choose inexpensive recreational activities.

____ Try to schedule your dates for the same time every week.

Part III: Protect Your Love Bank from Outside Threats

Follow the **Policy of Exclusivity**:

____ Avoid meeting the most important emotional needs, and having those needs met, by someone of the opposite sex other than your spouse, with special emphasis on affection, sexual fulfillment, intimate conversation, recreational companionship, and admiration.

____ Avoid contact with past lovers. Parenting issues with your ex-spouse should be managed by your spouse.

____ If you ever find yourself infatuated with someone other than your spouse, for whatever reasons, don't walk away—run! And tell your spouse.

14

Managing Resentment
and Restoring Trust

Jon felt betrayed, deceived, abandoned, and very angry when he discovered Sue's affair. After all, it was hatched with full knowledge of the pain it would inflict on him. It reflected a total disregard for Jon's feelings, someone whom Sue had promised to cherish and protect for life.

At first, Jon could not imagine ever having a normal relationship with Sue again. The image of Sue in bed with Greg was not only sickening to him, but also infuriating.

When Sue left him, she told him that she needed time to "sort out" her feelings. Jon knew what that meant—whoever made her feel the best, he or Greg, would win the prize of having her as a wife. The resentment that Jon felt seemed unbearable.

But there was more. After going back and forth a few times, trying to "get in touch" with her feelings, Sue tossed Jon out of his own home, separating him from his own children. And then, when the affair finally ended and Sue was rejected by her lover, she asked Jon to return. It wasn't Sue's choice; it was her lover's choice. Jon won by default.

Resentment doesn't begin to describe Jon's angry reaction to his entire ordeal.

But remarkably, the resentment that a betrayed spouse feels does not usually lead to divorce. In fact most betrayed spouses, like Jon, are willing to reconcile in spite of their resentment. However, when they try to rebuild their marriage, resentment and the fear of a new affair often threaten the ultimate success of the recovery.

Resentment is a normal reaction to someone who has made you suffer. It is the way your emotions warn you to avoid people who have hurt you in the past—they may hurt you again in the future! But resentment can also be an irrational reaction to something that is no longer a real threat. Resentment itself may become a greater obstacle to your happiness than what it is you resent.

Most couples I have counseled know how damaging their feelings of resentment are to their happiness and to the future of their marriage. But some seem unable to stop it—painful flashbacks seem to come out of nowhere. It's an interesting subject for a psychologist who is supposed to know how to help people control their thoughts and emotions. But, I must admit, this is a tough reaction to control, especially when memories are so distressing.

When couples attempt to reconcile after an affair, they may try to forgive and forget. But while all may be forgiven, all is not forgotten. It is impossible to forget a spouse's unfaithfulness, unless all memory goes along with it.

But one of the most remarkable discoveries of my career as a marriage counselor is that in spite of the memory of an affair, marriages can thrive.

Before infidelity actually happens, most couples think they could not continue in a marriage after an affair. The betrayal would be too painful. But what people think they will do with a wayward spouse isn't what they usually do.

Surprisingly enough, most couples eventually try to reconcile. Even though the memory can't be erased, they can survive the affair and create a thriving marriage. But what do they do with the resentment they feel as they try to reconcile?

The More Painful the Affair, the More Difficult Resentment Is to Overcome

Betrayed spouses almost always feel resentment. Both Jon and Lee were resentful about their spouse's affair. But Kevin's decisiveness in ending his affair early minimized Lee's suffering, and so her resentment was easier to overcome. On the other hand, Sue's vacillation between Greg and Jon, and then her eventual separation from Jon, greatly increased Jon's suffering and his resentment.

One of the reasons that I encourage a betrayed spouse to follow plan B (to avoid seeing or talking to the unfaithful spouse) when an affair does not end quickly is to minimize resentment when he or she tries to reconcile. The more contact there is between spouses during an ongoing affair, the more resentment there will be to overcome.

An emotional reaction to a painful event fades over time, as long as that painful event is not repeated.

An emotional reaction to a painful event fades over time, as long as that painful event is not repeated. But the more it is repeated, the more firmly fixed the memory becomes. In Jon's case, the painful events of Sue's affair were repeated again and again, and with each blow, his resentment was intensified.

I offered Jon and Sue a plan for reconciliation after the affair, but I knew the plan wouldn't work if Jon wasn't able to handle his feelings of resentment that were certain to accompany his reconciliation with Sue. If feelings of resentment are not dealt with correctly, they can ruin an otherwise stunning recovery.

Focusing on the Present and Future Can Help Diminish Resentment

As I've already said, it's impossible to completely forget a spouse's betrayal, but an effort can be made to avoid dwelling on that painful event. As we spend less and less time thinking about the betrayal, the memory of it will fade, along with the resentment we feel.

One of the reasons I do not encourage dwelling on the past as a part of marital recovery is that memories carry resentment along with them. If I'm not careful, a single counseling session can open up such a can of worms that the presenting problem gets lost in the flood of painful memories. If the goal of recovery is to "resolve" every past issue, that seems to me to be a good way to keep people coming to marriage counseling for the rest of their lives. I believe that resolving issues of the past is an insurmountable goal. We simply cannot learn to feel good about something that caused us great pain.

Instead, as I help people through marital recovery, the attention is focused on the present and the future, because we can do something about them. The past is impossible to change. Why waste our effort on things we have no control over when we can put that same effort into plans that will bring us a fulfilling future? Granted, it's useful to learn lessons from the past, but once we've learned the lessons, we should move on.

I believe this focus on the present and future is the best way to deal with feelings of resentment. Let me illustrate this point with Jon's experience.

When Jon expressed to me his resentment about the way Sue had treated him, I told him that we would put the issue of his resentment on hold as we focused on ways he and Sue could avoid making the same mistakes in the future. I asked him to trust my judgment and wait to see what happened to his resentment after his marriage had a chance to recover.

Only on rare occasions do I need to help a betrayed spouse overcome resentment after complete marital recovery. I've found that when marriages recover, using my concepts discussed in the previous chapters, resentment almost always fades away. And that's what happened to Jon. By postponing discussions about resentment, we put off an issue that took care of itself.

When spouses learn to become each other's greatest source of happiness (meet each other's most important emotional needs) and avoid being each other's source of unhappiness (overcome Love Busters), they greatly reduce the temptation of infidelity. And if they follow the extraordinary precautions I recommend, they make an affair essentially impossible, even if their marriage hits a temporary rough spot. In those cases resentment almost always fades away.

But if the narrow path for recovery that I've outlined in this book is not followed, romantic love will not be restored and the threat of another affair will persist. Then resentment, which is created by an unfulfilling marriage, will trigger resentment of the past affair.

While resentment almost always fades away when the plan I've recommended is followed, I've witnessed a few cases where resentment has persisted even after a full recovery. In those cases, I've looked for environmental triggers that keep a memory of the past alive. For example, one betrayed spouse I'd counseled whose marriage had fully recovered became resentful whenever she drove by an office building where her husband's lover had worked. The solution to her problem, of course, was to avoid that address.

While this client's problem was easily solved because there was only one environmental trigger, there are other spouses who find that a host of triggers keep reminding them of the affair. Their house, their car, their neighborhood, their grocery store, their church, their job, and even their friends trigger memories of the worst experience of their lives. In these cases, I've encouraged couples recovering from an affair to move to another city or state. While it's a difficult decision to make for most couples, I've found that it can be very effective in eliminating resentment for those who can't shake the recurring images of their spouse's affair.

One couple I counseled did move to another city after the wife's affair, and their recovery went very well. Thinking that they were now back on track and had nothing further to worry about, they moved back to their hometown. The wife's lover had left, and there was little risk for the affair rekindling. But as soon as they returned home, the husband's resentment returned along with their move. Environmental triggers kept his memories of the affair alive. In their case, a permanent move away from where the affair took place was the only way to eliminate those triggers.

Avoid Using Resentment to Justify Love Busters

Resentment and Love Busters usually work together. Love Busters, particularly selfish demands, disrespectful judgments, and angry outbursts, are ways we may be tempted to react once we feel resentful. In other words, resentment is a feeling that can make Love Busters seem justified.

There are many who react to their feeling of resentment by inflicting punishment on their spouse. They express their "feelings" as demands, disrespect, and anger. But it is abuse, pure and simple, disguised as the expression of honest feelings. No spouse has the right to punish the other spouse, and when resentment is felt, an abusive response must be avoided at all costs.

Some react to resentment by making demands on their spouse. Sadly, the tactic often works. The spouse will give in to the demand because he or she feels guilty about having had the affair. It's a Love Buster because it makes the spouse who must meet the demand very unhappy.

I received an email from a woman who had an affair ten years earlier. She said that whenever she and her husband had an argument or she was reluctant to have sex, he would bring up the fact that she had an affair. Being reminded of her affair would throw her off balance emotionally and make her feel guilty. To avoid his anger, and soothe her guilty feelings, she usually gave in to his demands.

No spouse has the right to punish the other spouse, and when resentment is felt, an abusive response is to be avoided at all costs.

I advised the woman to look her husband right in the eye and say to him, *Do you love me? Do you want me to love you? Do you want to spend the rest of your life with me? If the answer to any of those questions is yes, you should know that I will not give you what you want when you try to make me feel guilty. If you want to make love to me more often, let's negotiate. But what I did is in the past. Please do not bring it up again. I will not let you treat me this way because it will ruin my love for you.*

My advice to her husband was to avoid mentioning the affair again. When you keep bringing up your spouse's past mistakes, not only do you make your conversation incredibly unpleasant, but it cannot possibly lead to a resolution of a conflict that you may be discussing.

Sometimes when a person can't seem to let go of an unpleasant thought, it's because that thought is somehow helpful to him or her. Even though the thought is unpleasant, it gets the person something they want. The email writer's husband is a good example of this technique. The thought of his wife's affair was unpleasant but it was useful—bringing it up got him what he wanted. If the wife makes sure her husband never gets what he wants when he brings up the affair, he is more likely to let go of his resentment because it is no longer useful to him.

Jon was very tempted to use Love Busters in response to his feelings of resentment. But he understood how important it was for him to restore Sue's feelings of love for him and he knew that Love Busters would make her hate him, not love him. So he resisted selfish demands, disrespectful judgments, and angry outbursts, even when his feelings of resentment seemed overwhelming to him.

Restoring Trust

Without a doubt, an affair is the ultimate betrayal. An unfaithful spouse is fully aware of the suffering that the affair will inflict on their spouse, but feels justified in causing it to happen. It reflects a total disregard for their spouse's feelings, someone whom he or she had promised to cherish and protect for life.

And then there are the lies. Looking right at you and denying it all, getting angry that you would even think such a thing, and expressing shock that you would invade his or her privacy.

How can you ever trust someone who did all of that to you?

But the truth is, you may have more reason to trust your spouse after the affair than before it happened. How could I possibly come to that conclusion? It's all about understanding how trust is created and destroyed. Trust is the belief that your spouse won't do anything to hurt you and will be honest with you. It assumes a level of care that forms a protective envelope around you.

Trust is the belief that your spouse won't do anything to hurt you and will be honest with you.

I've introduced to you two policies that encapsulate the concept of trust. The first is the Policy of Joint Agreement: *Never do anything without an enthusiastic agreement between you and your spouse.* If your spouse's behavior reflects consideration of your interests and feelings, you have good reason to trust him or her to avoid doing anything to hurt you.

The second is the Policy of Radical Honesty: *Reveal to your spouse as much information about yourself as you know—your thoughts, feelings, habits, likes, dislikes, personal history, daily activities, and plans for the future.* This policy adds an important element to the protection that the Policy of Joint Agreement provides. It guarantees transparency so that nothing that your spouse does is ever hidden from you. By following this policy, your spouse gives you good reason to trust that what he or she tells you is the truth.

Before Sue's affair, Jon had trusted her to be honest with him and to avoid doing anything that would hurt him. More to the point, he had trusted Sue to avoid having an affair. But she had proven to be thoughtless.

Sue also had proven to be dishonest. She had looked right into Jon's eyes and lied to him. Then, faced with undeniable evidence, she had grudgingly and defensively admitted to one lie after another, but it was rarely accompanied by an apology. Considering her obvious failure to be honest and protect Jon's feelings, could he ever trust her again?

Before the affair, it's likely that your spouse was not following these two policies. You may have noticed incidents of independent behavior where your spouse did what he or she pleased knowing full well that you would not be happy with it. You may have also witnessed your spouse hiding the truth, or even giving you false information occasionally. Whatever the excuse would have been for violations of these two policies, you would have had little reason to trust your spouse at that time.

Just like Sue, your spouse has now proven to be incredibly thoughtless. He or she did nothing to protect your feelings, but instead, blatantly trampled over them. And your spouse was amazingly dishonest. Should you ever trust your spouse again?

One of the essential steps I recommend in my program of recovery after an affair is for spouses to learn to follow the Policy of Joint Agreement and the Policy of Radical Honesty so that they can create trust in each other. Those two policies define the meaning of trust, and by learning to follow them, they would have good reason to trust each other.

But I have counseled many unfaithful spouses who refuse to follow the Policy of Joint Agreement after an affair. In doing so, they admit that they are willing to let their spouse suffer so they can get what they want. When spouses of alcoholics complain that their drinking causes them to be unhappy, they drink anyway. Workaholics do the same thing. Their spouses' feelings and interests have little effect on their decisions. They do what they want, regardless of the negative effect on their spouses.

So if an unfaithful spouse is unwilling to follow the Policy of Joint Agreement, I explain to the betrayed spouse that they should not be trusted. Why? It's because we should trust only those who are willing and able to protect our feelings and interests. Someone unwilling to follow the Policy of Joint Agreement is also unwilling to do that. Even if a spouse has never had an affair, may not be an alcoholic, a workaholic, or any other kind of "holic," if that person is unwilling to follow the Policy of Joint Agreement it means that it's only a matter of time before an incredibly painful act of thoughtlessness will occur. That person should not be trusted.

In addition to refusing to follow the Policy of Joint Agreement, many of the unfaithful spouses I've counseled have also refused to follow the Policy of Radical Honesty. They don't want their spouse to know their passwords, their schedule, their cell phone records, and other personal information. And yet they tell me and their spouse that they've changed. Now we can trust them. But I tell them that they must prove their trustworthiness—and they're off to a very bad start.

Many unfaithful spouses have demanded that they be trusted. They argue that without that trust their marriage cannot thrive. They use that argument to avoid doing anything to regain trust. Instead of following the Policy of Joint Agreement, asking how their spouse would feel about their decisions, they insist that the spouse trust their judgment. They don't tell their spouse what they are doing in secret, but they want the spouse to believe that it is not anything harmful to the marriage. Demanding trust is simply a tactic to get away with further thoughtlessness and dishonesty.

Trust is not a marital obligation; it's a reaction to experience. It grows as each spouse shows himself or herself to be trustworthy. Marriage should begin with a commitment to be thoughtful and honest. Then, that commitment should be demonstrated with thoughtful and honest behavior. By following the Policy of Joint Agreement and the Policy of Radical Honesty consistently, a spouse would eventually prove his or her trustworthiness.

If someone who has a long history of dishonesty and thoughtlessness agrees to follow the Policy of Radical Honesty and the Policy of Joint Agreement, that person is on his or her way to becoming trustworthy, in spite of past history. As he or she learns how to be honest and thoughtful, and proves it again and again whenever conflicts arise, it's only a matter of time before trust is restored.

How could Jon be certain that Sue would not have another affair? How could he ever trust her again? He eventually trusted her because they built the foundation of their new lifestyle on the Policy of Radical Honesty and the Policy of Joint Agreement. Sue learned to be completely honest with Jon, and that prevented the creation of a secret second life—an essential ingredient of an affair. She was also firmly committed to taking Jon's feelings into account with every decision she made, thereby making another affair impossible.

Trust can be achieved in marriage, even after an affair. When honesty and thoughtfulness have been proven over a period of time (usually about two years), trust is created that does not have to be demanded. It comes naturally and effortlessly. And when it does, you have more reason to trust your spouse than you did before the affair took place.

Checklist for Managing Resentment and Restoring Trust

Overcome Resentment

___ Avoid mentioning the affair. Focus attention on the present and future.

___ Avoid using resentment to justify demands, disrespect, or anger when you have a conflict.

___ Avoid environmental triggers that remind you of the affair. Consider a move to avoid those triggers.

___ Allow about two years after your marriage has been restored for your resentment to fade.

Restore Trust

___ Follow the Policy of Radical Honesty and the Policy of Joint Agreement for two years.

___ Avoid demanding that your spouse trust you.

15

Sustaining Romantic Love

*A*fter Sue's affair had ended for good, and she and Jon had decided to reconcile, I asked them both to read and sign the Memorandum of Agreement that appears in appendix D. I would like you to do the same. Use information you have each reported in the Emotional Needs Questionnaire to list the five emotional needs you want each other to meet. Once they are identified in the form, sign two copies, one for each of you.

The Memorandum of Agreement is not to be taken lightly, because it commits you to put considerable effort and energy toward doing what would make you both happy and avoid what would make you unhappy. In other words, it requires you to be extraordinarily caring toward each other.

Jon and Sue agreed to the provisions in the Memorandum of Agreement. Without this commitment, I don't think their marriage would have survived because there were many moments, especially in the beginning, when they didn't feel like caring for each other. Instead, they wanted to hurt each other. But by keeping their eye on the goal and following the provisions of this agreement, they were able to overcome the destructive behavior that their emotions were encouraging them to do and replace that behavior with the care and consideration that their intellect knew was right.

If they had followed their short-term emotional instincts, in the end they would have continued to be emotionally devastated. But by following the direction of their intellect instead of their emotions, their negative emotional reactions eventually changed. Instead of finding each other repulsive, they found each other incredibly attractive.

It's a very important lesson for all of us to learn in life. If we let our emotions take charge of what we do, our lives will be very chaotic and unhappy. Our emotions tend to be very shortsighted. If we follow them to make decisions, they will usually lead us toward an unhappy and unfulfilling life. On the other hand, if we let our intelligence lead us toward long-term solutions to our problems, temporarily overlooking short-term negative emotional reactions, we ultimately tend to solve our problems and make our future happy and fulfilling.

Couples who try to reconcile without agreeing to the goals laid out in the Memorandum of Agreement usually fail to address the issues that created the affair in the first place. Before long they find themselves back in the same hopeless marriage, tempted to engage in another affair. But by making a commitment to the elements of this agreement, Sue and Jon were able to overcome the conditions that made her affair possible. And they created new conditions that affair-proofed their marriage.

At first, this lifestyle seemed very restrictive and unnatural. That's true of most things that are new—it takes awhile to get used to them. Not only were these policies new for Sue and Jon, they also contradicted most of their instincts. When they first married, they believed that they could trust their instincts. But their instincts had led them to disaster. The new lifestyle did something their instincts couldn't do—led Sue and Jon to marital recovery.

And what a recovery it was!

Sue's Side of the Story

I'll be honest with you. At first, I didn't believe that anything would do our marriage any good, but I went along with the plan because I had no other choice. I felt that I had nothing to lose by giving Jon a second chance. I figured I owed him at least that. But I had no feelings for him at all.

After about a week, I was feeling a lot better about my decision to live with Jon again and I started feeling less depressed. The time we spent together was not exciting but it wasn't unpleasant either. We weren't allowed to discuss my affair because I had already answered all of Jon's questions, and it would simply have been a rehashing of old news. That made everything much less stressful for me. I couldn't imagine ever loving Jon again but I began to see how we could live together, at least until the children were grown.

The goal for us was passion, something that I just didn't think would ever be possible. For the first few weeks, even though Jon was doing everything by the book, my feelings for him did not change. I thought of him as a friend, but not as a lover. Feeling that he was my friend was encouraging, though.

We continued to follow the plan and spent most of Jon's free time together. At times I resented giving Jon so much of my time but I figured it was a small price to pay to bring our family back together.

Then one day I really felt something for Jon. It was something I hadn't felt for him in years and I was very excited. We made love with passion for the first time in over two years, and I felt as if we had never been away from each other. In that moment, I loved Jon as much as I had ever loved Greg.

Unfortunately, the next day the feeling was gone. Before we had the Policy of Radical Honesty to follow, I would have lied to Jon about my loss of love for him. I used to think it was my marital obligation to tell him I loved him, but I didn't lie this time. I told him that my feelings for him were gone.

Jon handled the situation better than he would have before he knew about the Love Bank. He realized that my feelings for him would eventually return if he kept depositing love units. That put much less pressure on me, and I felt more at ease when we were together.

Then, a few days later, I felt love for Jon again. I was prepared for these cyclic feelings. I was told that when Jon deposited a certain number of love units into his account with me, that would trigger my feeling of love for him. When the account was above that point, I would be in love with him, and when it was below that point, the feeling of love would not be there.

And that's exactly what happened. As Jon kept depositing love units, slowly but surely the days I loved Jon increased in number, and the days I didn't love him decreased. I still have a hard time believing that love units could make such a difference in how I feel. I have always cared about Jon but I now understand that my feeling of passion toward him depends on how well he meets my emotional needs. And I also understand why I felt so much passion for Greg. It was because he had met my needs, not because he was really my soul mate. My real soul mate is the man I married, Jon. And now he stirs the same passion in me that Greg used to arouse.

I don't like to think about the nightmare I've been through. Even now, as I reflect on what happened, I start feeling depressed again. I am so grateful to Jon for waiting for me until I came to my senses. He could have left me because of everything I did. But instead, he kept reaching out to me, and that kept me from falling headlong into a pit that I don't think I could have ever survived. It was his strength that made up for my weakness, and I will always be grateful to him for his patience and commitment to me.

Jon's Side of the Story

At first, I was not sure I wanted Sue as my wife. The vision I had of her in bed with Greg made me sick to my stomach. But after I had a chance to think it over, I made a decision to do everything in my power to save our marriage.

At the time, I had no idea what that decision would cost me. And yet, in spite of all of the pain I've felt over the past two years, I would do it all over again for Sue. We both made mistakes and we had to pay for them. We ran the gauntlet and have come through it in love. We are much better people for it. I think our children will greatly benefit from the hard lessons we've learned.

When Sue finally invited me to come back to her, after Greg had left her for another woman, I was very bitter. She chose me because I was the only one left. Then, when I came back, she wouldn't even apologize. She blamed me for her affair. At the time I was ready to feed our new plan for recovery to the dog. I felt she owed me a lot and I expected her to welcome me with open arms. My friends thought I was crazy to take Sue back, and there were times that I thought they might be right.

But I had come this far, and I decided to give the plan a chance. My job was to keep my part of the bargain. Avoiding demands, disrespect, and anger was the hardest part. I bit my tongue so often I felt there would be none left.

Being with Sue was all it really took for me to redeposit all the love units that I had withdrawn from her Love Bank. Sue agreed to be with me at least fifteen hours every week, and that time together taught us how to become good friends again. Once her love for me was restored, I knew I could never take it for granted again.

I have finally learned how precious love is. The love Sue and I have for each other is what makes our marriage wonderful. Now that we've learned how to be in love with each other, I don't think either of us will make the same mistakes again.

In spite of what Sue put me through, I trust her now. That's because I know she loves me and she has put me first in her life. But I also know that following the Policy of Joint Agreement and Policy of Radical Honesty is what really keeps our marriage safe. It's keeping those policies that makes our trust in each other possible.

Review: The Plan for Marital Recovery

The plan for marital recovery that guided Jon and Sue to restore their love for each other also kept their marriage secure long after I counseled them for the last time. It made their marriage successful, and if you follow it, it will do the same for your marriage.

This plan is rather straightforward: *Make as many Love Bank deposits and as few withdrawals as possible.* And it makes perfect sense in marriage, because marriage is a relationship of extraordinary care. You select one person to cherish for the rest of your life. The goal of being that person's greatest source of happiness, and avoid being their source of unhappiness, shouldn't be difficult to understand.

But it's not only difficult for many couples to understand—it's even more difficult for them to do. Instead of making each other happy, they make each other miserable—the opposite of what marriage should be.

If you find my plan of recovery to be difficult to follow, you need it. You have developed habits that lead to marital unhappiness and divorce. And the more difficult it is for you, the more you need it. You've probably never been in the habit of making Love Bank deposits and avoiding withdrawals. You have a lot to learn.

On the other hand, if the plan is easy to follow, you've probably suffered a momentary lapse of care for each other, and it's simply a reminder of what you have done in the past to keep your love alive.

I use this plan to help couples recover after an affair, but technically, it's a plan to make any marriage successful. That's why my plan for marital recovery is so important to guide you in your quest for a fulfilling marriage. If you follow it, you will be as happy together as Jon and Sue are today. But if you don't follow it, you will certainly fail in your effort to recover after an affair. So, once more, let's review my plan for marital recovery that makes marriages successful.

One: Avoid Love Bank Withdrawals

You and your spouse were both born with the ability to hurt each other. And because you share your lives together, that ability can turn you into each other's greatest source of unhappiness. So if you want to be in love with each other, you should do everything in your power to resist the temptation to do anything that would make Love Bank withdrawals.

I've found that everything you can do that would upset each other can be classified into six categories: selfish demands, disrespectful judgments, angry outbursts, annoying habits, dishonesty, and independent behavior. These are habits that I call Love Busters because they destroy the feeling of love couples have for each other. But if you and your spouse agree to avoid being the source of each other's unhappiness, you will do whatever it takes to overcome these destructive tendencies. By eliminating Love Busters, you will not only be protecting your spouse from his or her greatest threat—you—but you will also be preserving your spouse's love for you.

My program of marital recover places special emphasis on two Love Busters: dishonesty and independent behavior.

Overcome Dishonesty by Following the Policy of Radical Honesty

Anything short of total honesty isn't honesty. Honesty means being truthful with your spouse about your positive and negative emotional reactions, personal history (which includes your weaknesses and strengths), your present schedule, and your thoughts and plans about future activities and objectives.

This description of honesty is spelled out in my Policy of Radical Honesty: *Reveal to your spouse as much information about yourself as you know—your thoughts, feelings, habits, likes, dislikes, past history, daily activities, and future plans.*

Self-imposed and persistent honesty with your spouse is essential to your marriage's safety and success. Honesty will not only bring you closer to each other emotionally, it will also prevent the creation of destructive behavior that is kept secret from your spouse—such as infidelity.

Overcome Independent Behavior by Following the Policy of Joint Agreement

The Policy of Radical Honesty gives you the facts you'll need to make your marriage successful and the Policy of Joint Agreement gives you the goal: *Never do anything without an enthusiastic agreement between you and your spouse.* Pure and simple, it encourages you to take each other's feelings and interests into account before you do anything.

One of the easiest ways to avoid Love Bank withdrawals is to follow the Policy of Joint Agreement. By following this policy you will be reminded that everything you do affects your spouse either positively or negatively, and by getting your spouse's enthusiastic agreement to what you do, you avoid behavior that will cause your spouse to be unhappy. The Policy will also encourage you to find mutually acceptable solutions to conflicts, instead of solutions that are good for one and bad for the other. By making mutually acceptable choices, you will create a lifestyle that both of you enjoy.

Independent behavior violates the Policy of Joint Agreement. When you behave independently, you act as if your spouse doesn't exist. Together with dishonesty, it's a necessary ingredient for infidelity because it's done in secret with total disregard for the betrayed spouse.

Two: *Make Love Bank Deposits*

You and your spouse fell in love with each other because you met each other's most important emotional needs, and the only way for you to stay in love is to keep meeting those needs. Even when the feeling of love begins to fade, or if it's gone entirely, it's not necessarily gone for good.

It can be recovered whenever you go back to being an expert at making Love Bank deposits.

To be an expert at meeting each other's most important needs, you must first know what your spouse's needs are, because they can change from time to time. Then you must learn to meet those needs in a way that is fulfilling to your spouse and enjoyable for you, too.

TAKE TIME TO MEET THE MOST IMPORTANT EMOTIONAL NEEDS BY FOLLOWING THE POLICY OF UNDIVIDED ATTENTION

The only way you can meet many of your spouse's important emotional needs is to give your spouse your undivided attention. And if you want it to be a reality instead of a hope, it must be a part of your schedule every week. I've written the Policy of Undivided Attention to remind couples of this important fact: *Give undivided attention to your spouse a minimum of fifteen hours each week, meeting each other's emotional needs of affection, sexual fulfillment, intimate conversation, and recreational companionship.*

I suggest that you (a) spend time alone when you give each other your undivided attention; (b) plan to schedule at least fifteen hours together each week; and (c) use this time to meet the emotional needs of affection, intimate conversation, recreational companionship, and sexual fulfillment. When these four needs are met every week, both husband and wife are happy. But when any of these needs are unmet, spouses usually feel frustrated and unfulfilled.

PROTECT YOUR LOVE BANK FROM OUTSIDE THREATS BY FOLLOWING THE POLICY OF EXCLUSIVITY

The Love Bank is an equal opportunity bookkeeper. Everyone you know has an account, and the way each person affects you is recorded. So when someone makes you feel very happy and fulfilled by meeting your most important emotional needs, enough deposits can be made in that person's account to trigger your feeling of romantic love. If you're not married to that person, you're in deep trouble. That's why you should guard your Love Bank from outside intruders. And the best way to place guards at the door is to follow my Policy of Exclusivity: *Meet each other's most important emotional needs exclusively.*

Since the most important emotional needs vary somewhat from person to person, you'll have to decide what needs make you feel happiest when met and make you feel the most frustrated when unmet. They're the needs that should be met exclusively in your marriage.

As mentioned in chapter 13, here are the precautions I recommend:

1. Affection is the symbol of care: *I care about the problems you face, and will be there for you if you need me.* It's a powerful need in all of us because we want to feel cared for by others. But it's particularly powerful for most women. When someone of the opposite sex expresses affection and meets that need, Love Bank deposits can be so huge that romantic love is triggered. So show each other affection throughout the day. But be very cautious about giving or receiving affection from anyone else of the opposite sex.

2. Deep down, you have always understood the importance of sexual exclusivity in marriage, even when you broke your vow. But now that you are restoring your marriage, and you are fully committed to never again sharing a sexual experience with anyone else, it should have special meaning to you. I want you to fully understand what that meaning of sexual exclusivity really is: *It's engaging in every sexual act or experience with your spouse and* only *with your spouse.* Pornography, strip clubs, and even masturbation should be completely off-limits. If you maintain a sexually exclusive relationship, it will help you keep your sexual experiences fresh and exciting, and will keep your Love Bank balances overflowing.

3. Intimate conversation is the emotional need that's met first in most affairs. It's the communication of personal topics, particularly the problems you are facing. Combined with affection, the expression of a willingness to help overcome those problems, intimate conversation helps make a marriage very fulfilling. But when it's shared with someone of the opposite sex outside of marriage, it destroys marriages. So whether face-to-face, by phone, by email, or by internet social network, avoid intimate conversation with anyone but each other.

4. When you are enjoying yourself the most, your spouse should be right by your side. So engage in your favorite recreational activities together. You should be each other's favorite recreational companions.

5. Compliments are common in life, and should be encouraged. But if the compliments are personal, about physical appearance, or if they reveal a special emotional attraction by someone of the opposite sex outside of marriage, run for cover.

6. Avoid contact with past lovers. It not only creates a risk of rekindling past relationships, but it's an offense to your spouse.

7. If you find yourself infatuated with someone other than your spouse, avoid that person, even if it's a longtime friend. Tell your spouse how you feel about that person and discuss what you can do to gracefully end your relationship.

Looking to the Future: Sustaining Romantic Love

Restoring your romantic love for each other is my immediate goal for your recovery, but sustaining your romantic love is the ultimate goal. After recovery, don't allow yourselves to become complacent, falling back into old habits where you neglect each other's emotional needs and start engaging in Love Busters. Instead, keep track of how you are doing in your marriage by taking time for an occasional evaluation.

To assist you with this evaluation, I've created six questions to determine if you are following the plan that helped restore your marriage. The answers to these questions can catch any slight relapse before it becomes serious enough to threaten your marriage.

I recommend that you schedule about thirty minutes on the first of each month to review these six questions:

1. Are we continuing to be experts at meeting each other's most important emotional needs?

2. Are we giving each other at least fifteen hours of our undivided attention each week, using the time to meet the needs for affection, sexual fulfillment, intimate conversation, and recreational companionship?

3. Are we protecting our Love Banks from outside threats?

4. Are we avoiding the Love Busters: selfish demands, disrespectful judgments, angry outbursts, annoying habits, dishonesty, and independent behavior?

5. Are we being radically honest with each other?

6. Are we making decisions with mutually enthusiastic agreement?

These questions can be answered to the affirmative quickly if you are still following the plan to care for each other. But if there is some reservation on the part of either of you, at least one of you is detecting a problem. Discuss the problem with each other and find a solution before any damage to your relationship takes place.

The most fulfilling part of marriage counseling is witnessing a couple's full recovery. I have seen thousands of couples move from a mutual loathing of each other to a deep emotional attraction and a strong bond.

I remind every couple that this renewed feeling of love was created by their willingness and ability to follow the narrow path that guided them. It was their ability to become each other's source of greatest happiness and to avoid being each other's source of unhappiness that made them successful.

But if they want this feeling to be sustained throughout their married life, they must continue to follow that narrow path. They must become experts at caring for each other, give each other undivided attention every week, avoid all Love Busters, be radically honest with each other, make their decisions with mutual enthusiasm, and protect their relationship from outside threats.

Sue and Jon, and Kevin and Lee, like many other couples, had wondered at first if they could ever heal from the emotional bruises that the affairs inflicted on them. But in the end, both marriages recovered completely. Both couples created marriages they had always wanted and needed, and the affair, while painful, did not keep them from a lifetime of love.

Checklist for Sustaining Romantic Love

___ If you have not yet completed and signed the Memorandum of Agreement (appendix D), do it now.

___ On a monthly basis, ask the following questions to help stay on the path of sustaining romantic love:

   ___ Are we continuing to be experts at meeting each other's most important emotional needs?

   ___ Are we giving each other at least fifteen hours of our undivided attention each week, using the time to meet the needs for affection, sexual fulfillment, intimate conversation, and recreational companionship?

   ___ Are we protecting our Love Banks from outside threats?

   ___ Are we avoiding the Love Busters: selfish demands, disrespectful judgments, angry outbursts, annoying habits, dishonesty, and independent behavior?

   ___ Are we being radically honest with each other?

   ___ Are we making decisions with mutual enthusiastic agreement?

Appendix A

The Most Important
Emotional Needs

Before you complete the Emotional Needs Questionnaire in appendix B, review the following ten most important emotional needs. For more information about these needs, I recommend reading my book *His Needs, Her Needs: Building an Affair-Proof Marriage.*

Affection: *The nonsexual expression of care through words, cards, gifts, hugs, kisses, and courtesies; creating an environment that clearly and repeatedly expresses care.*

Quite simply, affection is the expression of care. It symbolizes security, protection, comfort, and approval—vitally important ingredients in any relationship. When one spouse is affectionate to the other, the following messages are sent:

1. You are important to me, and I will care for you and protect you.
2. I'm concerned about the problems you face and will be there for you when you need me.

A hug can say those things. When we hug our friends and relatives, we are demonstrating our care for them. And there are other ways to show our affection—a greeting card, an "I love you" note, a bouquet of flowers, holding hands, walks after dinner, back rubs, phone calls, and conversations with thoughtful and loving expressions can all communicate affection.

Affection is, for many, the essential cement of a relationship. Without it many people feel totally alienated. With it they become emotionally bonded. If you feel terrific when your spouse is affectionate and you feel terrible when there is not enough of it, you have an emotional need for affection.

Sexual Fulfillment: *A sexual experience that is predictably enjoyable and frequent enough for you.*

Sex and affection are often confused, especially by men. Affection is an expression of care that is nonsexual and can be received from friends, relatives, children, and even pets. However, gestures that can show affection, such as hugging and kissing, that are done with a sexual motive are actually sex, not affection.

Most people know whether or not they have a need for sex, but in case there is any uncertainty, I will point out some of the most obvious symptoms.

A sexual need usually predates your current relationship and is somewhat independent of your relationship. While you may have discovered a deep desire to make love to your spouse since you've been in love, it isn't quite the same thing as a sexual need. Wanting to make love when you are in love is sometimes merely a reflection of wanting to be emotionally and physically close.

Sexual fantasies are usually a dead giveaway for a sexual need. In general, fantasies are good indicators of emotional needs, with your most common fantasies usually reflecting your most important needs. If you have imagined what it would be like having your sexual need met in the most fulfilling ways, you probably have a sexual need. The more the fantasy is employed, the greater your need. If you have a craving for sex—feeling very content when you have it often enough and very frustrated when you don't—you have a need for sexual fulfillment.

Intimate Conversation: *Talking about feelings, topics of personal interest, opinions, and plans.*

Intimate conversation is different from ordinary conversation. Its content focuses attention on very personal interests, problems, topics, and events.

It's intimate because you would generally not reveal such personal information to just anyone. Only those who seem to care about you and would be willing to help you think through the problems that you face are worthy of intimate conversation.

Men and women don't have too much difficulty talking to each other during courtship. That's a time of information gathering for both partners. Both are highly motivated to discover each other's likes and dislikes, personal background, current interests, and plans for the future.

But after marriage many women find that the man who would spend hours talking to her on the telephone now seems to have lost all interest in talking to her and spends his spare time watching television or reading. If your need for conversation was fulfilled during courtship, you expect it to be met after marriage.

If you see conversation as a practical necessity—primarily a means to an end—you probably don't have much of a need for it. But if you have a craving just to talk to someone, if you pick up the phone or go to your favorite internet social networking site just because you feel like talking, and if you enjoy conversation in its own right, consider intimate conversation to be one of your most important emotional needs.

Recreational Companionship: *Leisure activities with at least one other person.*

A need for recreational companionship combines two needs into one: the need to engage in recreational activities and the need to have a companion.

During your courtship, you and your spouse were probably each other's favorite recreational companions. It's not uncommon for women to join men in hunting, fishing, watching football, or other activities they would never choose on their own. They simply want to spend as much time as possible with the men they like and that means going where they go.

The same is true of men. Shopping centers are not unfamiliar to men in love. They will also take their dates out to dinner, watch romantic movies, and attend concerts and plays. They take every opportunity to be with someone they like and try to enjoy the activity to guarantee more dates in the future.

I won't deny that marriage changes a relationship considerably. But does it have to end the activities that helped make the relationship so compatible? Can't a husband's favorite recreational companion be his wife and vice versa?

If recreational activities are important to you and you like to have someone join you for them to be fulfilling, include recreational companionship on your list of needs.

Honesty and Openness: *Truthful and frank expressions of positive and negative feelings, events of the past, daily events and schedules, plans for the future; not leaving a false impression.*

Most of us want an honest relationship with our spouse. But some of us have a need for such a relationship because honesty and openness give us a sense of security.

To feel secure, we want accurate information about our spouse's thoughts, feelings, habits, likes, dislikes, personal history, daily activities, and plans for the future. If a spouse does not provide honest and open communication, trust can be undermined and the feelings of security can eventually be destroyed. We can't trust the signals that are being sent and we have no foundation on which to build a solid relationship. Instead of adjusting to each other, we feel off balance; instead of growing together, we grow apart.

Aside from the practical considerations of honesty and openness, there are some of us who feel fulfilled when our spouse reveals his or her most private thoughts to us. And we feel very frustrated when they are hidden. That reaction is evidence of an emotional need, one that can and should be met in marriage.

Physical Attractiveness: *Viewing physical traits of the opposite sex that are aesthetically and/or sexually pleasing.*

For many people, physical appearance can become one of the greatest sources of love unit deposits. If you have this need, an attractive person will not only get your attention but may distract you from whatever you're doing. In fact that's what may have first drawn you to your spouse—his or her physical appearance.

There are some who consider this need to be temporary and important only in the beginning of a relationship. After a couple know each other better, some feel that physical attractiveness should take a backseat to deeper and more intimate needs. But that's not been my experience, nor has it been the experience of many people I've counseled, particularly men. For many, the need for an attractive spouse continues on throughout marriage, and just seeing their spouse looking attractive deposits love units.

Among the various aspects of physical attractiveness, weight generally gets the most attention. However, choice of clothing, hairstyle, makeup, and personal hygiene also come together to make a person attractive. It can be very subjective, and you are the judge of what is attractive to you.

If the attractiveness of your spouse makes you feel great, and loss of that attractiveness would make you feel very frustrated, you should probably include this category on your list of important emotional needs.

Financial Support: *Provision of the financial resources to house, feed, and clothe your family at a standard of living acceptable to you.*

It may be difficult for you to know how much you need financial support, especially if your spouse has always been gainfully employed. But what if, before marriage, your spouse had told you not to expect any income from him or her? Would it have affected your decision to marry? Or what if your spouse could not find work, and you had to financially support him or her throughout life? Would that withdraw love units?

You may have a need for financial support if you expect your spouse to earn a living. But you definitely have that need if you do not expect to be earning a living yourself, at least during part of your marriage.

What constitutes financial support? Earning enough to buy everything you could possibly desire, or earning just enough to get by? Different couples would answer this differently, and the same couples might answer differently in different stages of life. But like many of these emotional needs, financial support is sometimes hard to talk about. As a result, many couples have hidden expectations, assumptions, and resentments. Try to understand what you expect from your spouse financially to feel fulfilled. And what would it take for you to feel frustrated? Your analysis will help you determine if you have a need for financial support.

Domestic Support: *Management of the household tasks and care of the children (if any are at home) that create a home environment that offers you a refuge from the stresses of life.*

Domestic support involves the creation of a peaceful and well-managed home environment. It can include cooking meals, washing dishes, washing and ironing clothes, cleaning house, managing the family calendar, and childcare. If you feel very fulfilled when your spouse does these things and very annoyed when they are not done, you have the need for domestic support.

The need for domestic support is a time bomb. At first it seems irrelevant, a throwback to more primitive times. But for many couples, the need explodes after a few years of marriage, surprising both husband and wife.

In earlier generations, it was assumed that all husbands had this need and all wives would naturally meet it. Times have changed, and needs have changed along with them. Now many of the men I counsel would rather have their wives meet their needs for affection or conversation, needs that have traditionally been more characteristic of women. And many women, especially career women, gain a great deal of pleasure when their husbands create a peaceful and well-managed home environment, or at least share that responsibility with them.

Marriage usually begins with a willingness of both spouses to share domestic responsibilities. Newlyweds commonly wash dishes together, make the bed together, and divide many household tasks. The groom welcomes his wife's help in doing what he had to do by himself as a bachelor. At this point in marriage, neither of them would identify domestic support as an important emotional need. But the time bomb is ticking.

When does the need for domestic support explode? When the children arrive! Children create huge needs—both a greater need for income and greater domestic responsibilities. The previous division of labor becomes obsolete. Both spouses must take on new responsibilities—and which ones will they take?

At this point in your marriage, you may find no need for domestic support at all. But that may change later when you have children. In fact, as soon as you are expecting your first child, you will find yourselves dramatically changing your priorities.

If you have children, and also have full-time careers, you and your spouse may both claim this need as among your five most important. In that case, sharing that responsibility may be the only way you can make each other happy.

Family Commitment: *Provision for the moral and educational development of your children within the family unit.*

In addition to a greater need for income and domestic responsibilities, the arrival of children creates in many people the need for family commitment. Again, if you don't have children yet, you may not sense this need, but when the first child arrives, a change may take place that you didn't anticipate.

Family commitment is not just childcare—feeding, clothing, or watching over children to keep them safe. Childcare falls under the category of domestic support. Family commitment, on the other hand, is a responsibility for the moral and educational development of the children, teaching them the values of cooperation and care for each other. It is spending quality time with your children to help them develop into successful adults.

Evidence of this need is a craving for your spouse's involvement in the moral and educational development of your children. When he or she is helping them grow, you feel very fulfilled, and when he or she neglects their development, you feel very frustrated.

We all want our children to be successful, but if you have the need for family commitment, your spouse's participation in family activities will make very large Love Bank deposits. And your spouse's neglect of your children will make noticeable withdrawals.

Admiration: *Being shown respect, value, and appreciation.*

If you have the need for admiration, you may have fallen in love with your spouse partly because of his or her compliments to you. Some people just love to be told that they are appreciated. Your spouse may also have been careful not to criticize you. If you have a need for admiration, criticism may hurt you deeply.

Many of us have a deep desire to be respected, valued, and appreciated by our spouse. We need to be affirmed clearly and often. There's nothing wrong with feeling that way. Even God wants us to appreciate Him!

Appreciation is one of the easiest needs to meet. Just offer a sincere compliment, and presto, you've made your spouse's day. On the other hand, it's also easy to be critical. A trivial word of rebuke can be very upsetting to some people, ruining their day and withdrawing love units at an alarming rate.

Your spouse may have the power to build up or deplete his or her account in your Love Bank with just a few words of admiration or criticism. If you can be affected that easily, be sure to add admiration to your list of important emotional needs.

Appendix B

Emotional Needs Questionnaire

© 1986, 2012 by Willard F. Harley, Jr.

Name _____ Date _____

This questionnaire is designed to help you determine your most important emotional needs and evaluate your spouse's effectiveness in meeting those needs. Answer all the questions as candidly as possible. Do not try to minimize any needs that you feel have been unmet. If your answers require more space, use and attach a separate sheet of paper.

Your spouse should complete a separate Emotional Needs Questionnaire so that you can discover his or her needs and evaluate your effectiveness in meeting those needs.

When you have completed this questionnaire, go through it a second time to be certain your answers accurately reflect your feelings. Do not erase your original answers, but cross them out lightly so that your spouse can see the corrections and discuss them with you.

The final page of this questionnaire asks you to identify and rank five of the ten needs in order of their importance to you. The most important emotional needs are those that give you the most pleasure when met and frustrate you the most when unmet. Resist the temptation to identify as most important only those needs that your spouse is *not* presently meeting. Include *all* your emotional needs in your consideration of those that are most important.

You have the permission of the publisher to photocopy the questionnaire for use in your own marriage.

1. **Affection.** The nonsexual expression of care through words, cards, gifts, hugs, kisses, and courtesies; creating an environment that clearly and repeatedly expresses care.

   A. **Need for affection:** Indicate how much you need affection by circling the appropriate number.

   If or when your spouse *is not* affectionate with you, how do you feel? (Circle the appropriate letter.)

   a. Very unhappy   c. Neither happy nor unhappy
   b. Somewhat unhappy   d. Happy not to be shown affection

   If or when your spouse is affectionate to you, how do you feel? (Circle the appropriate letter.)

   a. Very happy   c. Neither happy nor unhappy
   b. Somewhat happy   d. Unhappy to be shown affection

   B. **Evaluation of spouse's affection:** Indicate your satisfaction with your spouse's affection toward you by circling the appropriate number.

   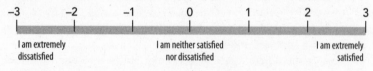

   My spouse gives me all the affection I need.   ☐ Yes   ☐ No

   If your answer is no, how often would you like your spouse to be affectionate with you?

   _____ (write number) times each day/week/month (circle one).

   I like the way my spouse gives me affection.   ☐ Yes   ☐ No

   If your answer is no, explain how your need for affection could be better satisfied in your marriage.

   _____

   _____

   _____

2. Sexual fulfillment. A sexual experience that is predictably enjoyable and frequent enough for you.

A. Need for sexual fulfillment: Indicate how much you need sexual fulfillment by circling the appropriate number.

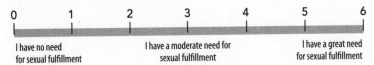

If or when your spouse *is not* willing to engage in sexual relations with you, how do you feel? (Circle the appropriate letter.)

a. Very unhappy   c. Neither happy nor unhappy

b. Somewhat unhappy   d. Happy not to engage in sexual relations

If or when your spouse engages in sexual relations with you, how do you feel? (Circle the appropriate letter.)

a. Very happy   c. Neither happy nor unhappy

b. Somewhat happy   d. Unhappy to engage in sexual relations

B. Evaluation of sexual relations with your spouse: Indicate your satisfaction with your spouse's sexual relations with you by circling the appropriate number.

My spouse has sexual relations with me as often as I need. ☐ Yes ☐ No

If your answer is no, how often would you like your spouse to have sex with you?

_____ (write number) times each day/week/month (circle one).

I like the way my spouse has sexual relations with me. ☐ Yes ☐ No

If your answer is no, explain how your need for sexual fulfillment could be better satisfied in your marriage.

_____

_____

_____

3. Intimate conversation. Talking about feelings, topics of personal interest/opinions, and plans.

   A. Need for intimate conversation: Indicate how much you need intimate conversation by circling the appropriate number.

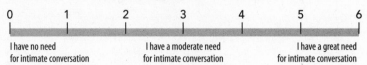

   If or when your spouse *is not* willing to talk with you, how do you feel? (Circle the appropriate letter.)

   a. Very unhappy   c. Neither happy nor unhappy

   b. Somewhat unhappy   d. Happy not to talk

   If or when your spouse talks to you, how do you feel? (Circle the appropriate letter.)

   a. Very happy   c. Neither happy nor unhappy

   b. Somewhat happy   d. Unhappy to talk

   B. Evaluation of intimate conversation with your spouse: Indicate your satisfaction with your spouse's intimate conversation with you by circling the appropriate number.

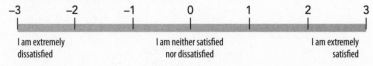

   My spouse talks to me as often as I need.   ☐ Yes   ☐ No

   If your answer is no, how often would you like your spouse to talk to you?

   _____ (write number) times each day/week/month (circle one).

   _____ (write number) hours each day/week/month (circle one).

   I like the way my spouse talks to me.   ☐ Yes   ☐ No

   If your answer is no, explain how your need for intimate conversation could be better satisfied in your marriage.

   _____

   _____

   _____

4. **Recreational companionship.** Leisure activities with at least one other person.

   A. **Need for recreational companionship:** Indicate how much you need recreational companionship by circling the appropriate number.

   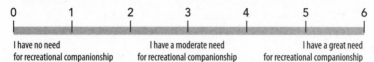

   If or when your spouse *is not* willing to join you in recreational activities, how do you feel? (Circle the appropriate letter.)

   a. Very unhappy   c. Neither happy nor unhappy

   b. Somewhat unhappy   d. Happy not to have my spouse join me

   If or when your spouse joins you in recreational activities, how do you feel? (Circle the appropriate letter.)

   a. Very happy   c. Neither happy nor unhappy

   b. Somewhat happy   d. Unhappy to have my spouse join me

   B. **Evaluation of recreational companionship with your spouse:** Indicate your satisfaction with your spouse's recreational companionship by circling the appropriate number.

   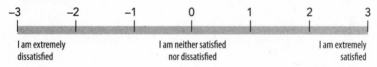

   My spouse joins me in recreational activities as often as I need.
   ☐ Yes   ☐ No

   If your answer is no, how often would you like your spouse to join you in recreational activities?

   _____ (write number) times each day/week/month (circle one).

   _____ (write number) hours each day/week/month (circle one).

   I like the way my spouse joins me in recreational activities.   ☐ Yes   ☐ No

   If your answer is no, explain how your need for recreational companionship could be better satisfied in your marriage.

   _____

   _____

5. Honesty and openness. Truthful and frank expression of positive and negative feelings, events of the past, daily events and schedule, and plans for the future; not leaving a false impression.

A. Need for honesty and openness: Indicate how much you need honesty and openness by circling the appropriate number.

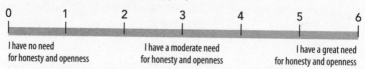

If or when your spouse *is not* open and honest with you, how do you feel? (Circle the appropriate letter.)

a. Very unhappy   c. Neither happy nor unhappy

b. Somewhat unhappy   d. Happy that my spouse isn't honest and open

If or when your spouse is open and honest with you, how do you feel? (Circle the appropriate letter.)

a. Very happy   c. Neither happy nor unhappy

b. Somewhat happy   d. Unhappy that my spouse is honest and open

B. Evaluation of spouse's honesty and openness: Indicate your satisfaction with your spouse's honesty and openness by circling the appropriate number.

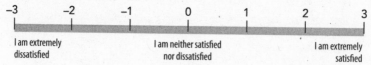

In which of the following areas of honesty and openness would you like to see improvement from your spouse? (Circle the letters that apply to you.)

a. Sharing positive and negative emotional reactions to significant aspects of life

b. Sharing information regarding his/her personal history

c. Sharing information about his/her daily activities

d. Sharing information about his/her future schedule and plans

If you circled any of the above, explain how your need for honesty and openness could be better satisfied in your marriage.

_____

_____

6. Physical attractiveness. Viewing physical traits of the opposite sex that are aesthetically and/or sexually pleasing.

A. Need for physical attractiveness: Indicate how much you need physical attractiveness by circling the appropriate number.

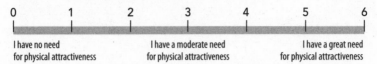

If or when your spouse *is not* willing to make the most of his or her physical attractiveness, how do you feel? (Circle the appropriate letter.)

a. Very unhappy   c. Neither happy nor unhappy

b. Somewhat unhappy d. Happy he or she does not make an effort

When your spouse makes the most of his or her physical attractiveness, how do you feel? (Circle the appropriate letter.)

a. Very happy   c. Neither happy nor unhappy

b. Somewhat happy   d. Unhappy to see him or her make an effort

B. Evaluation of spouse's attractiveness: Indicate your satisfaction with your spouse's attractiveness by circling the appropriate number.

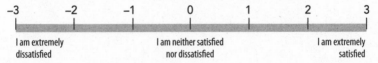

In which of the following characteristics of attractiveness would you like to see improvement from your spouse? (Circle the letters that apply.)

a. Physical fitness and normal weight

b. Attractive choice of clothes

c. Attractive hairstyle

d. Good physical hygiene

e. Attractive facial makeup

f. Other _____

If you circled any of the above, explain how your need for physical attractiveness could be better satisfied in your marriage.

_____

_____

7. **Financial support.** Provision of the financial resources to house, feed, and clothe your family at a standard of living acceptable to you.

A. **Need for financial support:** Indicate how much you need financial support by circling the appropriate number.

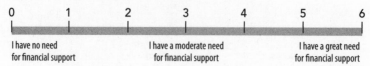

| 0 | 1 | 2 | 3 | 4 | 5 | 6 |

I have no need
for financial support

I have a moderate need
for financial support

I have a great need
for financial support

If or when your spouse *is not* willing to support you financially, how do you feel? (Circle the appropriate letter.)

a. Very unhappy   c. Neither happy nor unhappy

b. Somewhat unhappy   d. Happy not to be financially supported

If or when your spouse supports you financially, how do you feel? (Circle the appropriate letter.)

a. Very happy   c. Neither happy nor unhappy

b. Somewhat happy   d. Unhappy to be financially supported

B. **Evaluation of spouse's financial support:** Indicate your satisfaction with your spouse's financial support by circling the appropriate number.

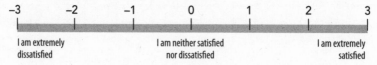

| −3 | −2 | −1 | 0 | 1 | 2 | 3 |

I am extremely
dissatisfied

I am neither satisfied
nor dissatisfied

I am extremely
satisfied

How much money would you like your spouse to earn to support you?

_____

How many hours each week would you like your spouse to work?

_____

If your spouse is not earning as much as you would like, is not working the hours you would like, does not budget the way you would like, or does not earn an income the way you would like, explain how your need for financial support could be better satisfied in your marriage.

_____

_____

8. **Domestic support.** Management of the household tasks and care of the children—if any are at home—that create a home environment that offers you a refuge from stress.

   A. **Need for domestic support:** Indicate how much you need domestic support by circling the appropriate number.

   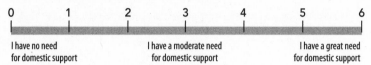

   | 0 | 1 | 2 | 3 | 4 | 5 | 6 |

   I have no need
   for domestic support

   I have a moderate need
   for domestic support

   I have a great need
   for domestic support

   If your spouse *is not* willing to provide you with domestic support, how do you feel? (Circle the appropriate letter.)

   a. Very unhappy   c. Neither happy nor unhappy
   b. Somewhat unhappy   d. Happy not to have domestic support

   If or when your spouse provides you with domestic support, how do you feel? (Circle the appropriate letter.)

   a. Very happy   c. Neither happy nor unhappy
   b. Somewhat happy   d. Unhappy to have domestic support

   B. **Evaluation of spouse's domestic support:** Indicate your satisfaction with your spouse's domestic support by circling the appropriate number.

   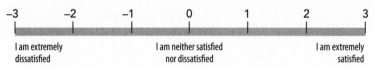

   | -3 | -2 | -1 | 0 | 1 | 2 | 3 |

   I am extremely
   dissatisfied

   I am neither satisfied
   nor dissatisfied

   I am extremely
   satisfied

   My spouse provides me with all the domestic support I need.
   ☐ Yes ☐ No

   I like the way my spouse provides domestic support.
   ☐ Yes ☐ No

   If your answer is no to either of the above questions, explain how your need for domestic support could be better satisfied in your marriage.

   _____

   _____

   _____

   _____

9. Family commitment. Provision for the moral and educational development of your children within the family unit.

A. Need for family commitment: Indicate how much you need family commitment by circling the appropriate number.

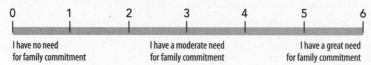

| 0 | 1 | 2 | 3 | 4 | 5 | 6 |

I have no need
for family commitment

I have a moderate need
for family commitment

I have a great need
for family commitment

If or when your spouse *is not* willing to provide family commitment, how do you feel? (Circle the appropriate letter.)

a. Very unhappy
b. Somewhat unhappy

c. Neither happy nor unhappy
d. Happy he or she is not involved

If or when your spouse provides family commitment, how do you feel? (Circle the appropriate letter.)

a. Very happy
b. Somewhat happy

c. Neither happy nor unhappy
d. Unhappy he or she is involved in the family

B. Evaluation of spouse's family commitment: Indicate your satisfaction with your spouse's family commitment by circling the appropriate number.

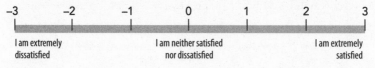

| –3 | –2 | –1 | 0 | 1 | 2 | 3 |

I am extremely
dissatisfied

I am neither satisfied
nor dissatisfied

I am extremely
satisfied

My spouse commits enough time to the family. ☐ Yes ☐ No

If your answer is no, how often would you like your spouse to join in family activities?

_____ (write number) times each day/week/month (circle one).

_____ (write number) hours each day/week/month (circle one).

I like the way my spouse spends time with the family. ☐ Yes ☐ No

If your answer is no, explain how your need for family commitment could be better satisfied in your marriage.

_____

_____

_____

10. Admiration. Being shown respect, value, and appreciation.

A. **Need for admiration:** Indicate how much you need admiration by circling the appropriate number.

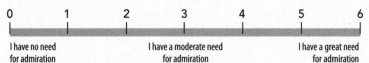

If or when your spouse *does not* admire you, how do you feel? (Circle the appropriate letter.)

a. Very unhappy   c. Neither happy nor unhappy

b. Somewhat unhappy   d. Happy not to be admired

If or when your spouse does admire you, how do you feel? (Circle the appropriate letter.)

a. Very happy   c. Neither happy nor unhappy

b. Somewhat happy   d. Unhappy to be admired

B. **Evaluation of spouse's admiration:** Indicate your satisfaction with your spouse's admiration of you by circling the appropriate number.

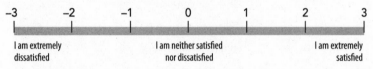

My spouse gives me all the admiration I need. ☐ Yes ☐ No

If your answer is no, how often would you like your spouse to admire you?

_____ (write number) times each day/week/month (circle one).

I like the way my spouse admires me. ☐ Yes ☐ No

If your answer is no, explain how your need for admiration could be better satisfied in your marriage.

_____

_____

_____

_____

Ranking Your Emotional Needs

The ten basic emotional needs are listed below. There is also space for you to add other emotional needs that you feel are essential to your marital happiness.

In the space provided before each need, write a number from 1 to 5 that ranks the need's importance to your happiness. Write a 1 before the most important need, a 2 before the next most important, and so on until you have ranked your five most important needs.

To help you rank these needs, imagine that you will have only one need met in your marriage. Which would make you the happiest, knowing that all the others would go unmet? That need should be 1. If only two needs will be met, what would your second selection be? Which five needs, when met, would make you the happiest?

_____ Affection

_____ Sexual fulfillment

_____ Intimate conversation

_____ Recreational companionship

_____ Honesty and openness

_____ Physical attractiveness of spouse

_____ Financial support

_____ Domestic support

_____ Family commitment

_____ Admiration

_____ _____

_____ _____

Appendix C

Love Busters Questionnaire

© 1992, 2013 by Willard F. Harley, Jr.

Name _____ Date _____

This questionnaire is designed to help identify your spouse's Love Busters. Your spouse engages in a Love Buster whenever one of his or her habits causes you to be unhappy. By causing your unhappiness, your spouse withdraws love units from your Love Bank, and that, in turn, threatens your romantic love for him or her.

There are six categories of Love Busters. Each category has its own set of questions in this questionnaire. Answer all the questions as candidly as possible. Do not try to minimize your unhappiness with your spouse's behavior. If your answers require more space, use and attach a separate sheet of paper.

When you have completed this questionnaire, go through it a second time to be certain your answers accurately reflect your feelings. Do not erase your original answers, but cross them out lightly so that your spouse can see the corrections and discuss them with you.

When you have completed this questionnaire, rank the six Love Busters in order of their importance to you. When you have finished ranking the Love Busters, you may find that your answers to the questions regarding each Love Buster are inconsistent with your final ranking. This inconsistency is common. It often reflects a less-than-perfect understanding of your feelings. If you notice inconsistencies, discuss them with your spouse to help clarify your feelings.

1. Selfish Demands: Attempts by your spouse to force you to do something for him or her, usually with implied threat of punishment if you refuse.

A. Selfish Demands as a Cause of Unhappiness: Indicate how much unhappiness you tend to experience when your spouse makes selfish demands of you.

| 0 | 1 | 2 | 3 | 4 | 5 | 6 |

I experience
no unhappiness

I experience
moderate unhappiness

I experience
extreme unhappiness

B. Frequency of Spouse's Selfish Demands: Indicate how often your spouse makes selfish demands of you.

_____ selfish demands each day/week/month/year.

(write number)   (circle one)

C. Form(s) Selfish Demands Take: When your spouse makes selfish demands of you, what does he or she typically do?

_____

_____

D. Form of Selfish Demands That Causes the Greatest Unhappiness: Which of the above forms of selfish demands causes you the greatest unhappiness?

_____

_____

E. Onset of Selfish Demands: When did your spouse first make selfish demands of you?

_____

_____

F. Development of Selfish Demands: Have your spouse's selfish demands increased or decreased in intensity and/or frequency since they first began? How do recent selfish demands compare to those of the past?

_____

_____

2. Disrespectful Judgments: Attempts by your spouse to change your attitudes, beliefs, and behavior by trying to force you into his or her way of thinking.

A. Disrespectful Judgments as a Cause of Unhappiness: Indicate how much unhappiness you tend to experience when your spouse engages in disrespectful judgments toward you.

```
0        1        2        3        4        5        6
|_____|_____|_____|_____|_____|_____|
I experience          I experience              I experience
no unhappiness        moderate unhappiness      extreme unhappiness
```

B. Frequency of Spouse's Disrespectful Judgments: Indicate how often your spouse tends to engage in disrespectful judgments toward you.

_____ disrespectful judgments each day/week/month/year.

(write number)   (circle one)

C. Form(s) Disrespectful Judgments Take: When your spouse engages in disrespectful judgments toward you, what does he or she typically do?

_____

_____

D. Form of Disrespectful Judgments That Causes the Greatest Unhappiness: Which of the above forms of disrespectful judgments causes you the greatest unhappiness?

_____

_____

E. Onset of Disrespectful Judgments: When did your spouse first engage in disrespectful judgments toward you?

_____

_____

F. Development of Disrespectful Judgments: Have your spouse's disrespectful judgments increased or decreased in intensity and/or frequency since they first began? How do recent disrespectful judgments compare to those of the past?

_____

3. Angry Outbursts: Deliberate attempts by your spouse to hurt you because of anger toward you. They are usually in the form of verbal or physical attacks.

   A. Angry Outbursts as a Cause of Unhappiness: Indicate how much unhappiness you tend to experience when your spouse attacks you with an angry outburst.

0	1	2	3	4	5	6

I experience
no unhappiness

I experience
moderate unhappiness

I experience
extreme unhappiness

   B. Frequency of Spouse's Angry Outbursts: Indicate how often your spouse tends to engage in angry outbursts toward you.

   _____ angry outbursts each day/week/month/ year.

   (write number)   (circle one)

   C. Form(s) Angry Outbursts Take: When your spouse engages in angry outbursts toward you, what does he or she typically do?

   _____

   _____

   D. Form of Angry Outbursts That Causes the Greatest Unhappiness: Which of the above forms of angry outbursts causes you the greatest unhappiness?

   _____

   _____

   E. Onset of Angry Outbursts: When did your spouse first engage in angry outbursts toward you?

   _____

   _____

   F. Development of Angry Outbursts: Have your spouse's angry outbursts increased or decreased in intensity and/or frequency since they first began? How do recent angry outbursts compare to those of the past?

   _____

   _____

4. Dishonesty: Failure of your spouse to reveal his or her thoughts, feelings, habits, likes, dislikes, personal history, daily activities, and plans for the future. Dishonesty is not only providing false information about any of the above topics, but it is also leaving you with what he or she knows is a false impression.

A. Dishonesty as a Cause of Unhappiness: Indicate how much unhappiness you tend to experience when your spouse is dishonest with you.

```
0        1        2        3        4        5        6
|        |        |        |        |        |        |
I experience              I experience              I experience
no unhappiness          moderate unhappiness      extreme unhappiness
```

B. Frequency of Spouse's Dishonesty: Indicate how often your spouse tends to be dishonest with you.

_____ instances of dishonesty each day/week/month/year.

(write number)   (circle one)

C. Form(s) Dishonesty Takes: When your spouse is dishonest with you, what does he or she typically do?

_____

_____

D. Form of Dishonesty That Causes the Greatest Unhappiness: Which of the above forms of dishonesty causes you the greatest unhappiness?

_____

_____

E. Onset of Dishonesty: When was your spouse first dishonest with you?

_____

_____

F. Development of Dishonesty: Has your spouse's dishonesty increased or decreased in intensity and/or frequency since it first began? How do recent instances of dishonesty compare to those of the past?

_____

_____

5. Annoying Habits: Behavior repeated by your spouse without much thought that bothers you. These habits include personal mannerisms such as the way your spouse eats, cleans up after him- or herself, and talks.

  A. Annoying Habits as a Cause of Unhappiness: Indicate how much unhappiness you tend to experience when your spouse engages in annoying habits.

```
0        1        2        3        4        5        6
|        |        |        |        |        |        |
```
I experience   I experience   I experience
no unhappiness   moderate unhappiness   extreme unhappiness

  B. Frequency of Spouse's Annoying Habits: Indicate how often your spouse tends to engage in annoying habits.

_____ occurrences of annoying habits each day/week/month/year.
(write number)   (circle one)

  C. Form(s) Annoying Habits Takes: When your spouse engages in annoying habits toward you, what does he or she typically do?

_____

_____

  D. Form of Annoying Habits That Causes the Greatest Unhappiness: Which of the above forms of annoying habits causes you the greatest unhappiness?

_____

_____

  E. Onset of Annoying Habits: When did your spouse first engage in annoying habits?

_____

_____

  F. Development of Annoying Habits: Have your spouse's annoying habits increased or decreased in intensity and/or frequency since they first began? How do those recent annoying habits compare to those of the past?

_____

_____

6. Independent Behavior: Behavior conceived and executed by your spouse without consideration of your feelings. These behaviors are usually scheduled and require thought to complete, such as attending sporting events or engaging in a personal exercise program.

A. Independent Behavior as a Cause of Unhappiness: Indicate how much unhappiness you tend to experience when your spouse engages in independent behavior..

0   1   2   3   4   5   6

I experience no unhappiness   I experience moderate unhappiness   I experience extreme unhappiness

B. Frequency of Spouse's Independent Behavior: Indicate how often your spouse tends to engage in independent behavior.

_____ occurrences of independent behavior each day/week/month/year.

(write number)   (circle one)

C. Form(s) Independent Behavior Takes: When your spouse engages in independent behavior toward you, what does he or she typically do?

_____

_____

D. Form of Independent Behavior That Causes the Greatest Unhappiness: Which of the above forms of independent behavior causes you the greatest unhappiness?

_____

_____

E. Onset of Independent Behavior: When did your spouse first engage in independent behavior?

_____

_____

F. Development of Independent Behavior: Has your spouse's independent behavior increased or decreased in intensity and/or frequency since it first began? How does recent independent behavior compare to that of the past?

_____

Appendix D

Memorandum of Agreement

© 1988, 2013 Willard F. Harley, Jr.

This Agreement is made the _____ day of _____, _____, between _____, hereinafter called "husband," and _____, hereinafter called "wife," whereby it is mutually agreed:

I. The husband and wife agree to avoid Love Bank withdrawals by protecting each other from Love Busters, with a special emphasis on avoiding dishonesty and independent behavior.

   A. To avoid Love Busters, the husband and wife agree to follow a course of action that identifies them, keeps a record of their occurrences, and eliminates them. The following Love Busters will not be tolerated in any form:

      1. *Selfish demands*: Attempts to force the other to do something with implied threat of punishment if he or she refuses. Selfish demands will be replaced with thoughtful requests.

      2. *Disrespectful judgments*: Attempts to change the other's attitudes, beliefs, and behavior by trying to force your way of thinking through lecture, ridicule, threat, or other means. Disrespectful judgments will be replaced with respectful persuasion.

      3. *Angry outbursts*: Deliberate attempts to hurt the other because of anger, usually in the form of verbal or physical attacks.

4. *Annoying habits*: Repeated behavior that unintentionally causes the other to be unhappy.

5. *Dishonesty*: Failure to reveal to the other correct information about emotional reactions, personal history, daily activities, and plans for the future. This also includes leaving a false impression.

6. *Independent behavior*: Activities of a spouse that are conceived and executed as if the other spouse did not exist.

B. To avoid dishonesty, the husband and wife agree to follow the **Policy of Radical Honesty:** *Reveal to your spouse as much information about yourself as you know; your thoughts, feelings, habits, likes, dislikes, personal history, daily activities, and plans for the future.* You will each provide:

1. *Emotional honesty*: Reveal emotional reactions, both positive and negative, to the events of your life, especially to the way your spouse is affecting you.

2. *Historical honesty*: Reveal information about your personal history, particularly events that demonstrate personal weaknesses or failures.

3. *Current honesty*: Reveal information about the events of your day, providing each other with a calendar of your activities, with special emphasis on those that may affect each other.

4. *Future honesty*: Reveal your thoughts and plans about future activities and objectives.

C. To avoid independent behavior, the husband and wife agree to follow the **Policy of Joint Agreement**: *Never do anything without an enthusiastic agreement between you and your spouse.* This policy guarantees that one spouse will not do anything to gain at the other's expense.

II. The husband and wife agree to make Love Bank deposits by meeting each other's most important emotional needs.

A. The husband and wife will identify and then learn to become an expert at meeting each other's five most important emotional needs. They will create plans to learn the habits that meet these needs, and then evaluate the success of their plans. Those needs may include the following:

1. *Affection*: The nonsexual expression of care through hugs, kisses, words, cards, and courtesies; creating an environment that clearly and repeatedly expresses care.

2. *Sexual fulfillment*: A sexual experience that is predictably enjoyable and frequent enough for you.

3. *Intimate conversation*: Talking about topics of personal interest, feelings, opinions, and plans.

4. *Recreational companionship*: Leisure activities with at least one other person.

5. *Honesty and openness*: Truthful and frank expressions of positive and negative feelings, events of the past, daily events and schedule, and plans for the future; not leaving a false impression.

6. *Physical attractiveness*: Viewing physical traits of the opposite sex that are aesthetically and/or sexually pleasing.

7. *Financial support*: Provision of the financial resources to house, feed, and clothe your family at a standard of living acceptable to you.

8. *Domestic support*: Management of the household tasks and care of the children (if any are at home) that create a home environment that offers you a refuge from the stresses of life.

9. *Family commitment*: Provision for the moral and educational development of your children within the family unit.

10. *Admiration*: Being shown respect, value, and appreciation.

The husband's five most important emotional needs ranked in order of importance are:

1. _____

2. _____

3. _____

4. _____

5. _____

The wife's five most important emotional needs ranked in order of importance are:

1. _____

2. _____

3. _____

4. _____

5. _____

B. The husband and wife will schedule time to meet the most important emotional needs by following the **Policy of Undivided Attention:** *Give your spouse your undivided attention a minimum of fifteen hours each week, using this time to meet important emotional needs.* They will do this by:

1. Insuring privacy, planning time together that does not include children, relatives, or friends so that undivided attention is maximized.

2. Using the time together to meet the needs of affection, sexual fulfillment, intimate conversation, and recreational companionship.

3. Committing to spend the number of hours that reflects the quality of the marriage: fifteen hours each week if the marriage is mutually satisfying, and more time if marital dissatisfaction is reported by either spouse.

4. Scheduling time to be together prior to each week and keeping a record of the time actually spent.

C. The husband and wife will protect their Love Banks from outside threats by following the **Policy of Exclusivity:** *Meet each other's most important emotional needs exclusively.* They will do this by:

1. Being cautious about giving or receiving affection from anyone else of the opposite sex.

2. Engaging in every sexual act or experience with each other and only with each other. Pornography, strip clubs, and even masturbation are completely off-limits.

3. Avoiding communication of personal topics, particularly the problems you are facing, with anyone else of the opposite sex, and limiting intimate conversation to each other.

4. Spending recreational time together, and being each other's favorite recreational companions.

5. Avoiding personal compliments, especially about physical appearance, to anyone else of the opposite sex.

6. Avoiding contact with past lovers.

7. Avoiding contact with anyone who triggers feelings of infatuation, and if it ever happens, telling the spouse about that person and discussing how to gracefully end that relationship.

In witness whereof, the parties hereto have signed this agreement on the day and year first above written:

Husband   Wife

Dr. Willard F. Harley, Jr., is a nationally acclaimed clinical psychologist, marriage counselor, and bestselling author. His popular website, Marriage Builders.com, offers practical solutions to almost any marital problem. He and Joyce, his wife of over fifty years, host a daily radio call-in show, *Marriage Builders Radio*. They live in White Bear Lake, Minnesota.

Dr. Jennifer Harley Chalmers is a licensed psychologist, author, international speaker, and marriage counselor. She and Phil, her husband of over twenty-eight years, live in the Philippines.

Dr. Harley and Dr. Chalmers have collaborated over the last twenty years to create and improve methods that restore love to marriage. Their primary focus has been the recovery of love after an affair.

The best book on marriage is now *better than ever!*

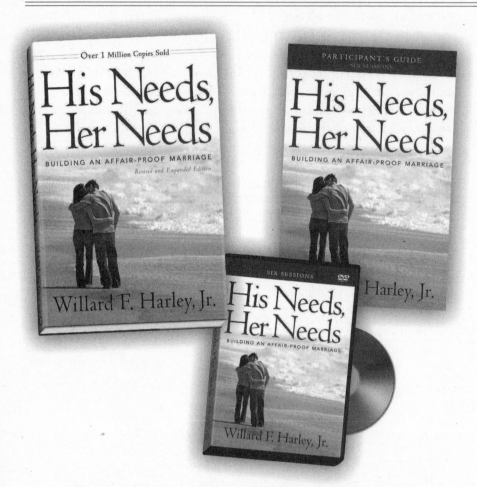

For over twenty-five years, *His Needs, Her Needs* has been transforming marriages all over the world. Now this life-changing book is the basis for an interactive six-week DVD study designed for use in couples' small groups or retreats, in pre-marital counseling sessions, or by individual couples.

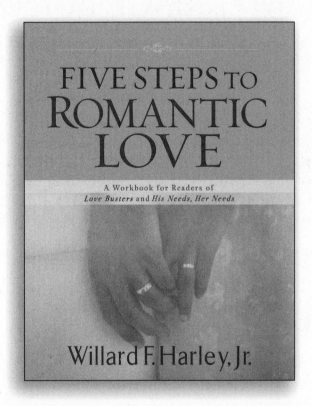

MARRIAGE BUILDERS®

Building Marriages To Last A Lifetime

At MarriageBuilders.com, Dr. Harley introduces you to the best ways to overcome marital conflicts and quickest way to restore love.

Read Dr. Harley's articles, follow the Q&A columns, interact with other couples on the Forum, and listen to Dr. Harley and his wife Joyce answer your questions on Marriage Builders® Radio. Learn to become an expert in making your marriage the best it can be.

Let Marriage Builders® help you build a marriage to last a lifetime!
www.marriagebuilders.com